INDUSTRIAL RELATIONS IN WEST GERMANY

A Case Study of the Car Industry

Industrial Relations in West Germany

A Case Study of the Car Industry

Wolfgang Streeck

St. Martin's Press · New York

ISBN 0–312–41519–2

Library of Congress Cataloging in Publication Data

Streeck, Wolfgang, 1946–
  Industrial relations in West Germany.

  At head of title: Policy Studies Institute.
  Bibliography: p.
  Includes index.
  1. Trade-unions—Automobile industry workers—Germany
(West) 2. Automobile industry and trade—Germany West—
Management—Employee participation. 3. Volkswagenwerk.
4. Collective bargaining—Automobile industry—Germany
(West) 5. Industrial relations—Germany (West)—Case
studies. I. Policy Studies Institute. II. Title.

HD6698.A8S77 1984   331′.04292′0943   83–40195
ISBN 0–312–41519–2

Contents

Foreword

This book is the product of a study that was initiated by the late Santosh Mukherjee, who worked at PEP and its successor, the Policy Studies Institute, from 1969 until his death in 1979. He was also from 1977 a research fellow at the International Institute of Management in Berlin, which collaborated with PEP (later PSI) in undertaking the study.

The study included an examination of railway unions, which was published as *Rail Unions in Britain and West Germany* (PSI Report No.604, 1982) by Peter Seglow, Wolfgang Streeck and Patricia Wallace. The research on unions in motor manufacturing was also undertaken in both Britain and Germany, and a report on the British research by Peter Seglow and Patricia Wallace is also being published by PSI. This book is about trade unionism in the German car industry. But both the British and the German research gained a great deal from the interaction between them and this has, among other things, enabled Wolfgang Streeck to write the book with knowledge of what aspects of the German experience are likely to be of particular interest to readers in Britain.

The present publication was not written primarily for an academic audience. It is an attempt to explain the functioning of the German industrial relations system to readers who are not necessarily industrial relations specialists. Thus, technical discussions and references to the literature have been avoided wherever possible. For readers who would like to know more about the subject, the book contains a bibliography of publications in English on German industrial relations.

We are grateful to the large number of people in the unions and elsewhere who agreed to be interviewed for the research. We are also grateful for financial support provided by the Anglo-German Foundation and by the International Institute of Management. Wolfgang Streeck wishes to express his thanks to PSI and the IIM for their patient support. Responsibility for the views expressed in the book lies entirely with him.

John Pinder
Director,
Policy Studies Institute

1 Introduction

In countries like Great Britain, Germany and Japan, the use of manpower in industry is subject to 'joint regulation' by employers, trade unions and the State. The institutional system in and through which such joint regulation takes place – mainly in the form of collective bargaining facilitated and complemented by legislation – is commonly referred to as a system of industrial relations. The structure of an industrial relations system determines, among other things, the ways available to organised labour to influence manpower use and to bring its interests to bear on managerial decisions on the organisation of production.

While for workers the institutionalised influence of trade unions on management is an important safeguard of their interests, from the perspective of management it imposes artificial rigidities on the organisation of work and these rigidities impede improvements in efficiency. This view is usually shared by the 'public' which, whenever its volatile attention is drawn to problems of industrial stagnation or decline, tends to blame 'excessive trade union power'. In this respect, co-determination in Germany has on the whole been afforded the same treatment as 'militant shop stewards' in Great Britain. In much of the public debate on industrial problems in highly industrialised countries low economic performance, and deficiencies in productivity in particular, are attributed to restrictions on management created by trade unions. Thus, a popular cure for industrial problems of all kinds is a restructuring of industrial relations which would lead to a 'roll-back' of trade union influence.

Undoubtedly, industrial change, and industry in general, are easier to manage if management does not have to overcome trade union resistance. Popular perceptions of the causes of industrial inefficiency and decline rest on this experience. The practical conclusion to which they lead is that efficiency is promoted by allowing unions as little influence on management as possible and, ideally, in preventing workers from organising in the first place. This presumes that unions, if given the power to do so, will always obstruct efficiency, and that 'industrial democracy' is inversely related to productivity. Successful economies, in a nutshell, are those that 'keep labour in its place'. Many in Britain, from both management and trade unions, have come to explain the superior performance of German industry in such terms.

While the proponents of the managerial position have been demanding similar restrictions on trade unions in Britain as they think exist in Germany, trade unionists in some countries have sometimes argued that for them unlike the Germans, the loss of democracy and the freedom to organise would be too high a price to pay for economic efficiency.

The most intriguing point about the 'union power obstructs efficiency' folklore is why it is so widely accepted. It is true that workers have interests opposed to industrial change. Almost inevitably change for them means insecurity, mobility, devaluation of skills and experience, and so on. But the same applies to management as well. Moreover, industrial efficiency is more likely to be in the interests of workers. The higher an industry's or company's productivity the higher their ability to pay, so that workers and their unions have a better chance to obtain high wages. Also, the more competitive a national economy, an industry or an employer, the safer, at least in the long run, are the jobs they have to offer. The expectation that trade unions will always try to prevent, obstruct or delay industrial change can thus hardly be based on their members' interests. The core theme of popular theories of trade unionism and industrial performance is, in fact, that while workers as such may indeed be positively interested in industrial efficiency, it is their organisations that are always directed against it, and it is through their organisation in trade unions that the interests of workers are turned against change and efficiency. In this sense, the theory of trade unionism as an obstacle to industrial change is not a theory of interests but a theory of organisation.

To be sure, there is nothing wrong with an organisational theory of collective behaviour in general and interest politics in particular. But to do justice to the role of organisation in the definition, selection and creation of collective interests, the argument should be followed through. If it is accepted that organisation can suppress the rather substantial interests of workers in industrial efficiency, the alternative possibility should also be considered that organisation might, in different circumstances, work in the opposite direction, that is, suppress or moderate, the interests vested in the *status quo*. The assumption is that it is not organisation as such that determines the substance of articulated interests but rather the form of organisation. Since the positive interests of union members in industrial change are certainly no less genuine than their negative ones, this assumption is not an unreasonable one.

If the possibility is accepted that organisational form may make a difference, trade union power and industrial efficiency are no longer mutually exclusive, and unions could be quite powerful without this leading to losses in industrial performance. While they would do their best to protect their members from the negative effects of change, unions if appropriately organised would be careful not to make change impossible, and the management objective of an efficient use of man-power would, in principle, be shared by them. In fact, such unions may become active proponents of change and rationalisation, and they may be prepared to co-operate with management and the State provided they are granted effective influence on the way in which change is brought about. It will be argued in this study that it is as a result of their organisational form and in response to the institutional structure of the industrial relations system of which they are part that German unions, like their counterparts in countries like Sweden and Austria, assume a positive attitude towards industrial change and efficiency. Moreover, we hope to show that contrary to widespread belief in Britain, they do so from a position of strength; it might even be said that it is exactly this strength that makes them willing and able to behave as 'responsibly' as they do.

How must industrial relations systems be structured, and how must trade unions be organised, to be receptive to industrial change? Mancur Olson (1976) has argued that one of the problems which present econ-omic theory is least equipped to handle is to account for differences in economic growth between developed industrial countries. The reason for this, Olson suggests, is that economists 'have been loth to turn (their) eyes away from (their) traditional line of vision' and thus failed to see a 'striking explanation' which is to do with 'the role of organized interest groups or associations – labour unions, professional associa-tions, farmers' organisations, lobbying groups, trade associations, and cartels'. Interests, according to Olson, are the more likely to be effec-tively organised the more specific they are and the smaller the groups that have common interests. The reason for this is that interest associ-ations generally cannot withhold the benefits of their activities from non-members. Most of what they achieve is a 'public good' in the sense that it 'goes to everyone in (the group they represent) if it goes to anyone in that group'. Organisations providing public goods, however, can support themselves only if they can 'either use some overt or covert form of coercion' on their beneficiaries to make them join or contribute, 'or else somehow offer some benefit in addition to their public good which . . . can be withheld from those who do not join'. Both are more likely to be possible if the group in question is small.

> One implication is that the largest and most scattered interests will presum-ably never be able to organize on a mass basis. Such groups as consumers, taxpayers, the unemployed, and the poor certainly have important common interests and surely would benefit substantially if there were effective mass organization working on their behalf. But it is hard to see how any organizer or political entrepreneur could (unless he had substantial assistance from the

government) manage to coerce such groups as consumers or poor people; these groups do not assemble at any one spot, the way the workers at a mine or factory do, and this means that nothing resembling the picket line would be feasible even if most consumers wanted it and the government would tolerate it. (Olson 1976)

The way these considerations relate to economic growth and efficiency is as follows. Olson argues that the interests represented by 'organised producer groups (cartels, unions) of the usual type and pattern' are normally and 'overwhelmingly' in conflict with the objective of general economic growth. The reason is that small groups 'can often gain substantially from a policy that reduces the output of the society as a whole, because they get most or all of the gains of the policy and bear little or none of the costs'. For example, organised producer groups 'systematically have an incentive to keep out new entrants to their industry or occupation' since this makes it possible for them to 'get away with producing less and charging more for it'. Or an organised group may 'have an incentive to block or delay the innovations that are the single most important source of economic growth' – for example, a union because its members 'might then need to find some other line of work', or 'a cartel-like trade association' because 'its less innovative members might suffer a competitive disadvantage'. However, Olson (1976) emphasises that 'it is not the common-interest organisation *per se* that inhibits growth', but rather the way it is structured:

> Suppose, contrary to fact, that some common-interest organization enrolled all producers, whatever their industry, or role, or region, in a given society. It normally could not be in the interest of the members of that organization to have policies that inhibit economic growth . . . Particular sub-groups of the membership might of course gain from a growth-inhibiting policy, but the output that was lost because of the policy could entail a loss for some other members of the organization: others would have to pay higher prices for the goods on which they spend their incomes, or wages, profits, or rents of other sub-groups would fall, or some combination of the foregoing would occur.

When this line of reasoning is applied to the problem of trade unionism and manpower use, the conclusion is that whether or not unions have an interest in preventing increases in industrial efficiency depends on the structure of their organisation.

> We should expect that organizations representing relatively specialized, narrow, or local interests would tend to be less inhibited about growth-repressing policies than broader organizations. The highly specialized craft union, for example, will find that, though its featherbedding will have the 'external diseconomy' of reduced national output, and will even typically reduce the aggregate earnings of the factors of production in the industry in which its members are employed, its own members bear such a minute share of these costs that the featherbedding may still be attractive. (Olson 1976)

This is different with what Olson calls 'encompassing organizations':

> An organization that represents all of the workers, or all of the firms, in an industry, will have reason to be somewhat less restrictive. A union that represented all manual workers in a country, or an organization that represented all major business, or a political party that represented all of some broad social group, such as the 'working class', would 'internalize' so much of the 'external diseconomy' of a growth-reducing policy that it is likely to do almost as much to promote growth as to prevent it. (Olson 1976)

In other words, the negative impact of trade unions on efficiency is lower the more the natural tendency of interest associations to be small, specialised and fragmented can be curbed, and the more successful a society is in organising its producer interests in broad, encompassing systems of collective representation. Olson's theory, and in particular its application to different countries, will be considered further in the final chapter.

Seen from a British perspective, the German system of industrial relations looks extremely encompassing. The number of unions in Germany is minute by British standards. Union members are organised regardless of their skill and occupation; craft unions making claims to job control or employment prerogatives do not exist; there are almost no unofficial strikes, and not many official ones either; collective bargaining is conducted on an industry-wide basis and well co-ordinated nationally; wage drift seems to be non-existent. British accounts of the German industrial relations scene often reflect bewilderment: where are the special interests of small groups that are so prominent in Britain? Why is there no sectional action – official or unofficial – by groups negatively affected by industrial change? If there is, for example, an erosion of wage differentials between unskilled and skilled workers, why do the skilled workers not take action to defend their position? If there is no such erosion, why do the unskilled not act to bring it about? How is it possible that there is only one industrial agreement covering the civil service, including national, Länder and local government, hospitals and refuse collection, universities and slaughtering houses, and, in effect, the railways and the postal service as well? How can strikes be so infrequent given the many different and specific problems which workers face in a dynamic economy? Why are strikes in Germany, if they do occur, always conducted on such a large scale, involving hundreds of thousands of workers from different occupations, skills, and types of plants at the same time and under one strategic 'master plan'?

As always when a phenomenon in a different country appears strange, 'cultural' explanations abound. Industrial tranquillity in Germany is attributed to the German's inborn, untameable *Arbeitslust*, their materialistic values, their masochistic pleasure in obeying their superiors, their continual fear of being punished by their ever-present State (that makes them carry identity cards), or to all these together. Likewise, the absence of sectional unions and sectional bargaining, and the German pattern of industrial action – 'large-scale industrial warfare' instead of small, spontaneous, autonomous 'hit and run' operations on the shop floor – are taken as an expression of the Germans' character-istic lack of individualism, their strong sense of collective discipline, and their traditional habit of following a Führer rather than thinking for themselves. Views like these can be found even in the writings of an author as sophisticated as Walter Kendall (1975) who maintained that 'certain attitudes of strongly inculcated upward deference seem deep-rooted in German society, not least the high value placed on security by the average worker and his unusually marked respect for received authority. For this the universities which until very recent years have survived largely unchanged in structure and outlook from the imperial regime, bear heavy responsibility'.[1]

According to one of the founding fathers of sociology, Max Weber, trying to explain differences between countries by 'national mentality' is 'but an admission of ignorance'. This may seem pretty strong lan-guage and to some it may even look like a typically German overstate-ment. To put the same point a little less polemically, what Weber probably meant to say is that explanations of other peoples' behaviour and institutions are better – that is, more universally acceptable – the less they are based on bizarre assumptions about motives and the standards of rationality underlying them. Social action, Weber argued, is 'explained' to the extent that it has been opened up to intuitive 'understanding', that is, that it is possible to see why any reasonable human being might act in a given way in a particular set of circum-stances. In this sense, the sociological concept of *Verstehen* rests on the 'universalistic' assumption that people are not totally different and that they have enough in common to be able, if they are willing to make the necessary effort, to change places and thereby 'understand' one another.

This book is making precisely this kind of effort. It is an attempt to explain the structure and the functioning of the German system of industrial relations, and of German trade unionism in particular, in terms of understandable, normal, interests and motives. Since it is not a historical study, it will not be concerned with the genesis of the institu-

---

[1] The way German authors at present write about the Japanese is not much different. For an extreme example of a book that easily qualifies as racist see Ariane Dettloff and Hans Kirchmann *Arbeitsstaat Japan: Exportdrohung gegen die Gewerkschaften* (Work-State Japan: Export Threat against the Unions), (Rowohlt, Hamburg, 1981). The authors are journalists who frequently write for trade union journals.

tions that are its subject. Rather, it undertakes to show why these institutions, however they may have come into being, continue to exist, why they are able to function and to grow and which rational interests, especially on the part of workers and trade unions, are accommodated by them and therefore sustain them. In this way, the study tries to show how an encompassing system of joint regulation and industrial interest representation works – how organisational structure, institutionalised influence and responsible behaviour of trade unions are related – and how this affects the use of manpower in industrial production.

As its empirical point of reference, the study takes the industrial relations system in the West German car industry. One reason for choosing the car industry is its obvious economic importance; it is one of the largest industries, and it occupies a key position in the German national economy. Moreover, and more importantly, there are strong contrasts between the industrial relations system and the economic development of the industry in Britain and Germany, and this will make the example particularly interesting for British readers.

The following chapter gives a description of the structure of trade unionism and collective bargaining in the German car industry. It is in particular concerned with the organisational mechanisms that make it possible for a centralised, monopolistic industrial union to function and maintain its unity. This theme is further developed in Chapter 3 which analyses the positive consequences of the legal institutionalisation of workplace industrial relations in Germany for the viability of industrial unionism. Chapter 4 shifts the focus of the discussion from 'structure' to 'influence'; it shows, using Volkswagen as an example, how trade union influence on company policy is institutionalised in the framework of industrial democracy (co-determination). Chapters 5 through 7 demonstrate how organisational structure and institutionalised influence result in the acceptance of 'responsibility': they present case studies on the role of trade unions and co-determination in decisions affecting the use of manpower, showing the organisational and institutional machinery described in Chapters 2 to 4 in operation. The first case study (Chapter 5) deals with the decision at Volkswagen in 1975 to lay off 20,000 workers; the second (Chapter 6) is on the decision at Volkswagen in 1976 to build an assembly plant in the United States; and the third (Chapter 7) describes the introduction at Volkswagen in late 1975 of a new policy on employment and overtime, comparing it to the policy on overtime adopted by the works council at the Opel factory in Rüsselsheim between 1975 and 1978. The last chapter (Chapter 8) pulls together some of the more general themes raised in this introduction and throughout the book. Among other things, it addresses the question to what extent the comprehensiveness of a system of industrial interest representation can be increased by State intervention; what impact a lasting economic crisis may have on encompassing institutions of industrial relations; and, above all, how different degrees of institutional inclusiveness are related to economic performance.

The largest, and for all practical purposes the only, union in the German car industry is the IGM (Industrial Union of Metal Workers). Other unions, notably the Deutsche Angestellten-Gewerkschaft (German Staff Union, DAG), may have small pockets of membership in some plants, but numerically and politically they are insignificant. Of the 566,000 workers employed in the German car industry in 1975, IGM organised about 69 per cent (76 per cent of the blue-collar workers, 41 per cent of the white-collar workers, 72 per cent of the men, 51 per cent of the women, and about 60 per cent of the workers from foreign countries). Because of the small size of the membership of competing unions, the density ratio of IGM can be regarded by and large as identical with the industry's overall level of unionisation.

IGM is an industrial union which organises, within its area of jurisdiction, all workers regardless of skill and occupational status. Like the other unions affiliated to the Deutscher Gewerkschaftsbund (DGB – German Trade Union Federation), IGM subscribes to the principle of 'one plant – one union' – or, more precisely, 'all plants in an industry – one union'. In fact, IGM represents an extreme case of industrial unionism in that its area of jurisdiction comprises, in terms of the German Standard Industrial Classification, not only one but 15 single industries which together are referred to in German as the *Metallindustrie* (in literal translation: the metal-working industry). Most important among these are the steel industry, the machine-tool industry, shipbuilding, the aerospace industry, the electrical engineering industry and, of course, the car industry. In 1975, IGM had $2\frac{1}{2}$ million members (1960: 1.8 million), that is, about one-third of all members of the then 16 DGB affiliates; this made IGM not only the largest union in the DGB but also, according to IGM literature, the largest union in the western world.

One consequence of the large size and the heterogeneity of IGM's area of jurisdiction is that no single industry can dominate the union's internal political life. Only 18.9 per cent of the IGM membership in 1975 were car workers (1960: 13.7 per cent). The four most important industries for IGM in 1975 – electrical engineering, mechanical engineering, cars and steel – together accounted for no more than 65 per cent of the membership. Although there are undoubtedly differences in the importance within the union between, say, the steel industry and the watch industry, nevertheless each industry is in a minority position and cannot by itself determine the union's policy.

Density ratios within IGM's area of jurisdiction show considerable differences by categories of members and by industries. In 1975, IGM organised about 73 per cent of the blue-collar workers in the *Metall-industrie*, 28 per cent of the white-collar workers, 66 per cent of the men, 41 per cent of the women, and 52 per cent of the foreign nationals. In 1961, the respective figures were 52, 16, 50, 25, and, in 1965, 23 per cent of the foreign nationals. As far as industries are concerned, density during the entire period was highest in old industries such as steel (1975: 88.4 per cent) and shipbuilding, and in predominantly blue-collar industries such as cars. Low density ratios existed in modern industries with relatively small-sized plants and a high proportion of highly skilled white-collar workers, and in industries using advanced technology even where plant size was large. An example of the first category is the machine-tool industry which in 1975 had a density ratio of 37.7 per cent; an example of the second is electrical engineering with a density ratio of only 30.7 per cent.

Since the re-establishment of the German union movement after the second world war, IGM has always been the leading union in the DGB. While this is partly because of its sheer size and the significance of its industries for the German economy, other factors have also played a role. Under the leadership of Otto Brenner (1949–1972), IGM became the foremost stronghold of the 'traditionalist' wing of the DGB which, among other things, continued to demand the nationalisation of important branches of industry. Politically, IGM at this time was seen as one of the centres of opposition against the restoration of capitalism during the Adenauer era. This made it the natural target of conservative anti-unionism. In addition, the IGM for a long time has been the 'wage leader' of the German union movement. (After 1970, this role went for a while to the Union of Public Service Workers, ÖTV.) In the yearly wage negotiations, the other unions usually let IGM settle first and then try to settle at approximately the same rate of increase. This, together with its unmistakable political and ideological position, made the IGM in the eyes of many observers the most important political force in the West German union movement, more important than even its peak organisation, the DGB.

Organisational structure of IGM: central and local level
IGM's territorial organisation today has three main levels: the district, the regional and the national level. In 1976, IGM had 168 districts, with an average membership of 15,365, and 10 regional organisations. Every three years, districts elect delegates for the general conference. Full time officials are permitted to stand for election and are often elected.

In advance of the general conference, regional conferences are called which elect regional committees. Posts on the regional committees are not paid, and regional committee members are either voluntary officials or full time officials from the districts. The leader of the regional organisation, the regional secretary, is a full time official who is appointed by the national executive. In addition to electing the regional committee, regional conferences discuss the matters which are to be put forward at the general conference and nominate candidates for various national offices. The general conference can pass resolutions on all aspects of union policy, and with a majority of two-thirds of its members it can amend the rulebook. Furthermore, at each general conference all members of the national executive, including the chairman, have to stand for re-election.

The national executive of IGM consists of 30 members. Eleven of these, among them the chairman and the vice-chairman, are paid by the union; they form the 'standing committee' of the executive. Each of the paid executive members supervises one or more departments of the central executive office and is politically responsible to the full executive for the work of his departments. Departments are assigned to executive members by the full executive after it has been elected by the general conference. The standing committee generally convenes once a week. About four times a year, the full national executive meets to consider, on the basis of reports prepared by the standing committee, matters of more general importance. Both the standing committee and the full executive are presided over by the chairman of the union.

Although the unpaid members of the national executive are by no means without influence, the real power at the national level clearly lies with the standing committee and, in particular, with the chairman. Partly, this is due to the fact that the standing committee has, through the regional secretaries, a strong influence on the nomination of the unpaid executive members. Another reason, and perhaps the most important one, is the standing committee's control over the central bureaucracy (which in 1976 consisted of 171 full time officials, not counting the technical and administrative staff) and over the union's day-to-day business. Meetings of the full executive are prepared in detail by the chairman's staff. The standing committee and the chairman, assisted by their departments, determine the agenda of national executive meetings and usually are able to structure the issues in such a way that the final decisions conform with their intentions. In fact, although it has happened that the chairman has been outvoted in the standing committee, it is almost inconceivable that the standing committee would in an important matter be over-ruled by a majority vote in the full executive.

After each general conference, all elected district officials have to stand for re-election. First, members in each district elect assemblies of delegates which for the ensuing three years will represent the membership in the district. Each assembly then elects a district executive. (Three years later before the next general conference, assemblies elect delegates to the general and the regional conference.) The posts of chairman of the executive – the 'district secretary' – and, depending on the size of the district, of the vice-chairman and the treasurer, are full time; the rest of the executive consists of lay members. Both the full time and the lay executive members have to be confirmed in office by the national executive before they can take up their posts.

Districts have their own rulebooks. However, district rules have to keep within the framework set by the national rulebook and by the 'model district constitution' (*Musterortsstatut*) issued by the national executive. To ensure conformity with national standards, district rules need the national executive's approval before they come into operation. This limits local discretion considerably. In addition, the national executive has the right to alter the demarcation of districts 'when necessary or expedient' and to remove local executives and replace them for a limited time by appointed officers if a district is in violation of national rules.

Indicators of centralisation abound in IGM's formal organisational structure. The rule book in various places expressly limits the powers of local and regional bodies in favour of the national executive. Thus, Section 14,4(a) states that the district executive governs the district 'in accordance with the directions, guidelines and powers given to it by the national executive on the basis of the decisions of the general conference . . . and of the national executive'. Similarly, according to Section 15,1, decisions made by the district assembly of delegates are binding on the members of the district only 'insofar as they are not in conflict with decisions of the general conference and the national executive'. As to the regional level, the regional secretaries are characterised in Section 16, 4 as the 'representatives of the national executive in the regions' who have to 'perform their function in line with its instructions'. This is of particular importance with regard to collective bargaining since the regional secretaries are the leaders of the union's negotiating teams. Regional conferences are to be called 'by the regional secretary at the instance of the national executive'; their agenda is set up 'by the regional secretary in agreement with the national executive' (Section 17,5), and their possible role is limited by Section 17,1 to 'the effective support of the regional secretary, the discussion of tactical matters and the facilitation of the implementation of decisions made by the general conference'.

A telling indicator of the distribution of authority in IGM's organisational structure is the terminology used in the rulebook. Unlike other unions, at IGM the German word for executive, *Vorstand*, is used only for the national executive. At the regional level – in the *Bezirke* – the rulebook does not speak of a *Bezirksvorstand* but only of a *Bezirkskommission* (regional committee). Similarly the district executive is called *Ortsverwaltung* (local administration) instead of *Orts-* or *Verwaltungsstellenvorstand*. In both cases, the use of the language serves to emphasise the lack of political autonomy of such bodies and their subordination to the directive power of the national executive (which is referred to in the rulebook not as *Bundesvorstand* or *Hauptvorstand* as in other unions but just as *der Vorstand*).

To understand this no doubt extraordinary distribution of organisational authority, it is necessary to look at the system of collective bargaining in the German metal-working industry and its underlying ideology. This will be done in the ensuing part of this chapter. Following this, another important aspect of organisational structure will be discussed, the relationship between the union at the workplace ('internal workplace organisation') and the industrial ('external') union. The final part of the chapter returns to the general problem of 'encompassing organisations'; it raises the question of why car workers in Germany agree to their interests being represented by a general union for the entire metal-working industry, rather than by a specialised car workers union (or even specialised unions for different groups of car workers).

Union structure and collective bargaining

With the exception of the steel industry and the metal artisan establishments which are separate industrial bargaining units, IGM negotiates one encompassing collective agreement for its entire area of jurisdiction including the car industry. Among the industries covered are the foundry industry and the musical instruments industry, but on the whole, the economic sector to which the agreement applies corresponds by and large to what is called in Britain the 'engineering industry'. Formally, negotiations for the industry are conducted, and separate agreements are signed, by regional officials in 11 territorially defined 'bargaining districts'.[1] However, all important decisions by the IGM negotiators require approval by the national executive. As a last resort, the national executive even has the power to take the negotiations out of the hands of the regional officials and negotiate directly with the central executive of the employers association. While this frequently happened in the 1960s, since the wave of unofficial strikes in 1969 the IGM leadership prefers to have formally decentralised negotiations. However, the results reached in the regional bargaining districts usually differ only in minor details, and wage rounds affect incomes and conditions in all regions in about the same way.

From a British perspective, the most striking aspects of this system of collective bargaining are its high degree of centralisation on the one hand and the large size and the extreme heterogeneity of the bargaining units on the other. Both correspond to the basic philosophy underlying industrial unionism in Germany. Although historically, centralised negotiations may have been forced upon the unions against their will by strong employers associations, after the second world war it was largely because of union pressure that the centralised bargaining system was re-established and maintained. It is interesting to note that IGM in its present organisational form is much older than the corresponding employers association for the engineering industry, *Gesamtmetall*, which was formed only in the early 1960s.[2]

The political concept behind the option of German unions for a centralised and integrated pattern of collective bargaining can be summed up in the notion of 'solidaristic wage policy'. German industrial unions believe that the benefits of economic progress should be shared by all members of the working class alike, and that a worker should suffer as little as possible from his employer's failure to provide for a high level of productivity. Wage increases and improvements of conditions should therefore be negotiated in one common round of negotiations for all workers together rather than for individual groups of workers separately. The latter would mean that workers in a strong market position – skilled workers, workers in regions where labour was scarce or in industries and enterprises with high productivity – would obtain higher increases than less privileged workers so long as their special circumstances hold. By including the strong and the weak in one encompassing system of collective bargaining, industrial unionism aims to effect a redistribution of bargaining power and hence of income, in favour of the weak. Unions are aware that such a system may prevent workers in economically privileged positions from exploiting their opportunities in the market to the fullest extent, and that such workers may have to content themselves with less than what they could get were they permitted to act on their own. On the other hand, those in weak positions, as a result of their integration into a more encompassing bargaining unit, have a chance to get more than they would have been able to get otherwise. It is this 'averaging out' of market power among the different groups of the 'working class' which provides the rationale for a centralised system and internally heterogeneous units of collective bargaining.

The centralisation of collective bargaining at IGM is organisationally supported and protected by the dominant position in the bargaining process of professional union officers. In comparison with British unions, IGM has always been a highly professional organisation and has become more so in recent years. Centralisation and professionalism are closely related in industrial unions in that professionalism helps to

insulate a union's political process against pressures from the membership, and especially from sectional groups within it. Lay leaders are
closer to the sectional interests of specific trades, occupations, industries, or companies than full time officers. While the first have to be
responsive to the interests of the particular groups of members by
whom they have been elected, full time officers are primarily interested
in the organisation as a whole and in protecting it against internal or
external disruption. The more influence lay officials or members have
in comparison to full time officers, the more difficult becomes the task
of containing and managing internal interest heterogeneity. Moreover,
full time officials are far more likely than lay leaders to enforce the
compromises negotiated by the organisation on behalf of the members.
The greater the role of professional staff in an industrial union, the
more 'industrial' the policy of the union can become, and the more
effective the union will be in aggregating the special interests of its
members and in transforming them into a united strategy.

The area in which the influence of full time officers at IGM is most
safely established is collective bargaining. All important decisions in
this field are made by the central executive which is dominated by full
time officials. Also, all negotiations with employers, at whatever level,
are conducted by negotiating committees which, although they generally do have lay members, are always led by professional union officers
who act as the principal negotiators and are in this capacity bound by
national policy guidelines.

This is not to say that there is no participation of lay members in
collective bargaining, but the final decisions always lie with full time
officers. Extensive provisions are made in IGM's organisational structure to draw the membership into the bargaining process as early and as
deeply as possible without thereby jeopardising the control of the
central and professional leadership. Yearly wage rounds are opened
months before the actual start of negotiations by a statement of the
central executive describing the economic situation and outlining possible issues and demands. This statement is then discussed at all levels
of the union organisation and particularly in meetings at the workplaces. While the executive and the full time officers in this period try to
mobilise support for the strategy suggested in the initial statement,
members may, and often do, pass resolutions demanding changes.

The result of the discussion phase is summed up by the regional pay
committees (*Tarifkommissionen*) which are elected every three years by
the regional conferences and which consist of about 50 to 120 members.
Pay committees are composed of delegates from all union districts in
the region and include representatives from all major plants and occupational groups; their composition is regulated by guidelines issued by
the national executive. Resolutions of pay committees are not binding;

technically they are treated as recommendations to the national executive which the latter can choose to adopt or to turn down.

After the initial discussion phase, each regional pay committee together with the national executive sets up its official list of demands to be presented to the employers. Regional claims normally differ slightly from each other because of – mainly technical – differences in existing regional agreements. Basically, however, the fact that the executive has the final decision and the pay committees are limited to an advisory function ensures that all regions follow the same line.

During the actual negotiations, pay committees participate in two ways. The first is that they continue to advise the negotiators and the national leadership on all strategic and tactical matters of importance. Whenever decisions on such matters come up, the national executive and the pay committee meet to consider the available options and to search for a consensual solution. Although, in principle, the executive could act without the agreement of the committee, in practice this rarely happens. Secondly, while pay committees have no direct part in the actual negotiations with the employers, they have the right to nominate some of their members, usually two or three, on to the negotiating committee where they join the regional secretary and the other full time officers appointed as negotiators by the executive. Negotiating committees are always chaired, and negotiations are conducted, by a full time officer who normally is the regional secretary. The role of the pay committee delegates during the negotiations is to ensure that the chief negotiator follows the guidelines agreed upon between the national executive and the full pay committee.

In the final phase of a negotiating round, the pay committee may be in continuous session for several days and nights, hearing reports from the negotiators and advice from the national executive, and making recommendations on the further instructions to be given to the negotiators. During this process, which may involve decisions on taking a strike vote, asking for arbitration, or calling a strike, the lay members on the negotiating committee play an important part as it is often their reports from the bargaining table by which the pay committee is most effectively influenced. However a wage round goes and whatever steps are taken by the union during its course, the final collective agreement is signed by the executive only after the results have received majority approval of the pay committee.[3] It is not infrequent that the negotiating committee does not get such approval and is sent back by the pay committee to the bargaining table. On the other hand, the dominant role of the full time officials in the actual negotiations, the composition of the pay committees, their close involvement in the bargaining process, the right of the national executive to reject demands by pay committees for a strike vote or a strike, and the need for comparable agreements to be reached in all regions ensure that the national executive always gets its way. In this sense, rank-and-file participation in collective bargaining in IGM has aptly been characterised as 'quasi-participation', serving important functions for internal consensus-building while leaving the discretion of the professional leadership unimpaired.

Territorial and workplace organisation

The components of trade union organisational structures can be classified in two main categories: those that are based on, and geared to, specific places of work ('production units'), and those that represent workers in a specific territory regardless of their workplace. Examples of the first kind are shop stewards, plant branches, shop steward combine committees, full time company organisers, national union trade groups, and union executive committees composed of trade group representatives. Examples of the second kind are local branches, district, regional and national secretaries and their office staff, general conferences, and district, regional and national committees to the extent that their members are selected regardless of the plant, company and industry in which they are employed.

Workplace-based and territorially-based union structures differ with regard to the type of interests they emphasise. While workplace-based structures tend to give preference to interests that are related to the special conditions in particular companies, plants, or workshops, territorially-based structures are more likely to express those (general) interests of the members that are independent of specific workplaces. This is not to say that territorial union structures do not or cannot take account of workplace-related differences of interest. Nor is it to say that organisational elements representing different workplaces cannot arrive at a joint definition of interest and a corresponding strategy. Nevertheless, territorially constituted union structures are more likely to leave aside workplace-related special interests and enforce a general policy on all members regardless of their place of work. Likewise, workplace-based union organisations are likely to give more freedom of expression to workplace-specific interests and to achieve a lower degree of interest-political centralisation and unification than territorially constituted structures.

Union organisations differ greatly with regard to the relative importance of the two categories of organisational elements. In one extreme case, a union may have no territorially constituted structure at all, and its organisation may be exclusively geared to a particular company ('company unionism'). While most unions do have some bodies with a territorially defined jurisdiction, these units may consist of elected representatives of specific companies or industries ('trade groups') and may thus be more workplace than territorially oriented. At the opposite end of the continuum, it is possible to envisage a union all of whose organisational elements are constituted according to members' place of residence rather than place of work, and which do not have any workplace-specific subunits. Adjacent to this extreme type would be a union which, whilst it does maintain workplace-based elements, does not grant them political autonomy or decision-making authority.

The structure of IGM almost ideally exemplifies the relationship between the workplace-based and the workplace-independent elements of union organisation which is necessary for the smooth functioning of industrial unionism. It has been seen that collective bargaining on behalf of IGM is conducted by full time officers, and that all decisions relating to it are made by the national executive, not for single plants or companies but for territorially defined bargaining regions. There are a few exceptions to this practice, one of which is Volkswagen (see p. 46). Production units do not at any point in the bargaining process serve as constituent units of organisational decision-making. When a strike vote is taken, for instance, its result always applies to an entire bargaining region as a whole; a plant which votes differently from the rest of the region is not exempt from the consequences of the regional vote. Even the members of the pay committees, as we have seen, are not elected at their workplaces but by the regional conferences which are constituted on a territorial rather than on a workplace basis.

The same principles apply to the structure of IGM districts. All decision-making bodies of the district are formed on the basis of members' place of residence, and no district official is elected or appointed by workplace or company. This holds even for the members of the assembly of delegates whose constituencies continue to be the local branches although these otherwise have lost almost all of their previous functions. The result is that no local IGM official is committed to workplace-related special interests, and no political mandate is based on the specific conditions in particular places of work.

Generally, throughout IGM's organisational structure formal political authority never originates from a specific workplace; it is always based on territorial units. All elections of workplace union representatives require confirmation by district organisations which are constituted along strictly territorial lines. Workplace-based union bodies have advisory functions only; they cannot make decisions and they even lack the formal right to pass resolutions for consideration by the district assembly. Nor are there decision-making bodies above plant level that are constituted on a workplace basis – for example, councils of workplace representatives from a particular region or industry. Any such structure would be in conflict with the IGM rule book and the model district constitution and would be abolished by the national executive using its constitutional reviewing powers. Where supra-plant bodies of workplace representatives exist at the district level, they are formed on a purely residential basis and again have no power to make decisions. Finally, while there are occasional conferences of workplace representatives at district, regional or national level – some of which are even specialised by industry – they are called only on specific issues by the respective territorially-based executive committee which determines their agenda and whose representatives always have the chair. Conferences of this kind are strictly limited to an advisory function and have no machinery and no standing organisation of their own.

The principle that divisions among members by production units are not to be represented in internal decision-making structures, applies to all levels and segments of IGM's organisation and is observed not only with respect to individual plants and firms but also to industries. Although IGM organises no less than 15 different industries, none of these – except for the steel industry and the metal artisan establishments both of which have their own industrial agreements – is permitted to form a separate subunit within IGM which could be used as a basis for internal representation of industry-specific interests. All decisions on union policy are made in bodies whose members come, or could come, from any of the industries organised. Not a single official, voluntary or full time, is elected or appointed by an industry or is exclusively concerned with the problems of one industry or company. Except for a few loose working groups chaired by officials from headquarters which are strictly limited to technical functions, there is nothing in the organisational structure of IGM that corresponds to the distinctions between, or the specific interests of, individual industries. Thus, the only body within IGM which is specialised on the automobile industry – in addition to occasional 'car workers conferences' held by the national executive – is a standing working group of a small number of workplace representatives from the big car plants which produces yearly comparisons of wages and conditions. As the different car companies use different payment systems, making comparisons of this kind is a very difficult task requiring considerable expertise. Accordingly, the work of the group is highly technical, and as a rule its members are not the leading figures of their workplace organisations but rather specialists on wages, piece rates, and other payment systems. Another indication of the non-political status of the group is that it is chaired by an appointed official from the collective bargaining department at IGM headquarters.

The need in industrial unions for external control over the workplace is particularly evident when it comes to strikes. Employers are, at least in the long run, prepared to recognise as a representative of their workers, anybody who has the power to organise a strike. A union seeking an industry-wide collective agreement must therefore be able not only to call an industry-wide strike but also to guarantee industrial peace once the agreement has been concluded. If a union cannot give this guarantee, the employer will sooner or later negotiate with whoever can, and the union's objective to regulate wages and conditions industry-wide will be frustrated. It is the extent to which an industrial union can establish an effective 'strike monopoly' that enables it to gain a 'bargaining monopoly' for its industry. If the industrial union as an organisation above the level of individual firms is not in a position to end or prevent unauthorised strikes by single groups of members or by the workforce of individual establishments – for example, those that are particularly profitable – the result will be a fragmentation of the bargaining system and the breakdown of industrial unionism.

Car workers in IGM: the problem of integration

Why is it that normally car workers in Germany accept representation by a general union for the entire engineering industry which does not even have a special car workers trade group? How is it possible that car workers are content with an industrial agreement applying not just to their industry but to 14 others as well? Contrary to outward appearance, the existing structure is by no means taken for granted among IGM members and officials, and its preservation requires considerable effort and vigilance on the part of the IGM leadership. Among car workers, there is sometimes considerable dissatisfaction with the results of comprehensive and 'solidaristic' bargaining. One way in which this expresses itself among car industry workplace leaders is in an occasional 'flare-up' of resentment against their industry or company, being covered by the same agreement as 'any small village blacksmith' (interview). More important is the recurrent talk among trade unionists in the big car manufacturing companies on the possible advantages of a 'separate car industry unit within IGM' (interview), a special car industry agreement negotiated by IGM, or even a German UAW.[4] How tenuous the stability of an organisation like IGM really is, is indicated by the fact that even the most trivial events of this kind are taken extremely seriously by the leadership and are reacted to immediately and decisively. This applies in particular to the car industry where a separate union would be perfectly viable as an organisation.

An often-heard explanation why the separatist tendencies among car workers have up to now been too weak to get their way is economic. Normally, the business cycle of the car industry in Germany lags behind that of the rest of the engineering industry. When the other industries are already picking up, the car industry tends to be still declining, and when the others are moving into a recession, the car industry may still be booming. According to national IGM officials, it is only in the latter case, and never in the former, that car workers are reported 'to play with the idea of a German UAW'. As soon as the car market starts to decline, car workers begin to benefit from belonging to the same bargaining unit as the rest of the engineering industry, and their desire for an autonomous organisation or a separate agreement disappears. While workers in the car industry may occasionally have to lend some of their bargaining power to other metal workers, experience has taught them – so it is argued – that they are always paid back through the union when they need support themselves. This is said to explain why their separatism never becomes strong enough to prevail over the forces of cohesion represented by the national executive.

Although this undoubtedly goes some way to account for IGM's past success in protecting its organisational unity, it is not the complete picture. While national IGM officials insist that it is economically rational for car workers to remain in the general engineering industry bargaining system, this can be, and in fact is, seen rather differently by car workers' representatives. For example, throughout the latest car boom from 1975 to 1980 the industry was economically in far better condition than the rest of the engineering sector. As a result, the industrial agreements for the engineering industry as a whole continued to remain behind what could have been negotiated in separate agreements for the car industry. Moreover, since the German car industry in the 1960s and 1970s had above-average growth rates in spite of occasional recessions, many trade unionists from car firms feel that on balance a separate agreement would have been more advantageous for them, and that possible future losses resulting from independent bargaining in periods of low growth would easily be offset by the possible gains in boom periods. That this view is not entirely unrealistic is indirectly confirmed by the swiftness with which the national headquarters act to quell anything that might become the beginning of a separatist movement among car workers. The fact that such organisational controls are necessary at all is an indication that, at least in this case, economic interests are by themselves not sufficient as a motive for 'solidaristic' action, and that voluntary integration of encompassing bargaining units based on rational self-interest is a highly precarious arrangement. If this is true, however, then the obvious success of a formally voluntary organisation like IGM in preserving unity among its heterogeneous interest groups raises the question by what extra-economic factors such success has been made possible.

German trade unions, and above all IGM, differ from their British counterparts by their high degree of organisational and operational centralisation, their capacity to aggregate a wide range of diverse special interests into a common, 'solidaristic' policy, their successful

maintenance of a monopoly of representation in their respective juris-
dictions, and their ability to prevent dissatisfied groups among their
members breaking away and forming independent, competing unions.
All these characteristics are related to, and based upon, effective control by the territorial, external union organisation over the internal union
at the workplace. To understand German industrial unionism, the ability
of the external union in Germany to establish and protect its political
primacy over the union at the workplace has to be explained. The
principal assumption here is that such primacy is unlikely to develop
voluntarily. Especially against the background of the British experience, it is suggested that the establishment of stable external control
within trade unions requires more organisational resources than a
voluntary organisation can muster on its own. For industrial unionism
to become organisationally possible, the internal control capacities of
trade unions must be increased and reinforced by supporting institutions. To explain why German trade unions manage so spectacularly to
prevent organisational fragmentation and to protect their (external)
strike monopoly the system of industrial relations in which they operate
must be examined. The hypothesis put forward here is that the dis-
tinguishing characteristics of German trade unions, and their successful solution of the organisational problems of 'solidaristic' industrial
unionism, can for a large part be accounted for by the existence in
Germany of a statutory system of interest intermediation at the workplace – the so-called *Betriebsverfassung*. It is to the form in which
industrial relations at the workplace are institutionalised in Germany
and the relationship of this to the organisational structure of West
German trade unions, that the next chapter will be devoted.

Footnotes

[1] Formally, there are 14 separate bargaining districts but for the four northern-
most districts negotiations are conducted jointly and only one joint agreement
is signed.

[2] *Gesamtmetall* is a confederation of 14 regional employers associations for the
Metallindustrie. Its area of organisation is identical with the area covered by the
Metallindustrie industrial agreement. Unlike IGM, *Gesamtmetall* does not
cover employers in the steel industry or the metal artisan establishments.

[3] There is an important exception to this principle. When an agreement has
been reached in one bargaining district and after it has been accepted by the
appropriate pay committee, the national executive may order the other
regional union negotiators to sign an identical agreement with their counterparts from the employers' side provided, of course, that the employers are
prepared to do so. This order has binding power and the 'pilot agreement' is
transferred to other bargaining districts even if the respective pay committees
vote against it.

[4] Meaning, of course, the American United Automobile Workers' Union.

3 Union Organisation and the Works Constitution

The central characteristic of the German system of industrial relations is the existence of a statutory system of interest representation which is formally independent of the unions. Workers in establishments with more than four employees are entitled under the Works Constitution Act (*Betriebsverfassungsgesetz*) to elect, as a representative of their interests, a works council (*Betriebsrat*, see Section 1 of the Works Constitution Act in the Appendix). Election procedures, duration of office, size and composition of the works council and the rights and obligations of works councils in relation to the employer are all regulated by the Act (Sections 9, 10, 12, 14 and 20). Works councils are elected for three years by secret ballot, and all employees are eligible to vote and may stand for election regardless of union membership. To enable a works council to function, the law obliges the employer to recognise it as the representative of the workforce and to provide it with the necessary resources – in particular, office space, secretarial assistance, and release from work (Sections 37, 38, and 40).[1]

German trade unionism cannot be adequately understood without a proper understanding of the functioning of the works councils system in general and of the relationship between unions and works councils in particular. Under the law, the jurisdiction of unions and works councils are carefully separated. Unions, which are formally voluntary organisations, can act as agents of collective bargaining but works councils as statutory bodies are in law prevented from doing so. Instead, they have a number of legal rights to consultation and co-determination.[2] On subjects that legally come under co-determination, the employer in principle requires the assent of the works council before he can act. Works councils can negotiate with their employer so-called 'works agreements' (*Betriebsvereinbarungen*) which are the equivalent in the domain of co-determination to collective agreements (*Tarifverträge*) in the domain of collective bargaining. Both are legally binding. If works council and employer cannot reach agreement on an issue under co-determination, a conciliation and arbitration procedure is provided for by the Works Constitution Act (Section 76). Also, if a works council feels that its employer is interfering with its legal rights, it can take the employer to the Labour Court.[3] Similarly an employer can appeal to the Labour Court if he feels that works councils are acting *ultra vires*.

The relationship between unions and works councils varies by subject areas. On some subjects, works councils perform and even mono-polise tasks which in other industrial relations systems, for example, in Britain, would be considered genuine union tasks. In other areas, works councils are legally bound to co-operate with the unions and have to abide by, and even to execute, their policies. In still others, they are legally forbidden to take any action whatsoever, which in effect amounts to a legal protection of unions against works council inter-ference and competition.

The main field in which the first kind of relationship prevails is that of manpower policy at the workplace. While the statutory consultation and co-determination rights of works councils in this area (Sections 75, 80, 87, 90–92, 99, 102, 111, 112) do not formally prevent workplace union organisations from taking up the same matters independently in the context of collective bargaining, the legally guaranteed recognition of works councils on these matters makes this *de facto* impossible. The prevailing, and for all practical purposes the only, mode of joint regula-tion with regard to the use of manpower in Germany is, for this reason, not collective bargaining but co-determination.

An example for the second type of relationship between unions and works councils is the legal obligation for works councils under the Works Constitution Act (Section 80,1,1) to ensure that industrial agreements are enforced. Where industrial agreements exist, it is the legal obligation of works councils to observe them. Matters which are regulated by industrial agreement are in principle beyond the jurisdic-tion of co-determination. Works agreements which contradict indus-trial agreements are legally void. Co-determination, in this respect, complements rather than takes the place of collective bargaining, with the works council system functioning in effect as an implementation mechanism for industrial union policy at the workplace.

Thirdly, works councils are in no circumstances permitted to negoti-ate over wage rates (Section 77,3). Wage rates are reserved as a subject of negotiation exclusively to collective bargaining and thus to the unions. An important exception is the application of industrial agree-ments on piece rates in individual establishments. In this respect, collective agreements usually include a clause which 'expressly autho-rises the making of supplementary works agreements' (Section 77,3). The actual role of works councils in wage bargaining is, however, much more complex than is indicated by the Act and this subject will be taken up later in more detail.

The reason why the distinction between co-determination and collec-tive bargaining, statutory and voluntary mechanisms of interest repre-sentation, works council and union is so crucial is its bearing on the right to strike. While trade unions, as participants in collective bargain-ing, have in principle the right to call strikes, works councils as agents of statutory co-determination, have not (Section 74, 2 and 3). Within the framework of co-determination, disputes between workers and employers are resolved not through industrial action but exclusively through conciliation, arbitration and Labour Court awards. Matters of joint regulation on which workers are, by law or *de facto*, represented by their works council cannot therefore become the subject of a strike. Such matters are, in particular, the use of manpower at the workplace and the application and supervision of industrial agreements at the level of individual establishments. The main purpose of the present chapter is to explore the implications of this legal situation for the structure of trade union organisation and the conduct of industrial relations in Germany.

At the outset, it may be useful to discuss briefly a question which suggests itself especially from a British perspective. This is why employers are prepared to make significant concessions to works councils when the councils cannot support their demands by industrial action. One answer is that German employers do not, any more than British employers, like 'outsiders' to interfere with the running of their establishments. Since an unresolved disagreement with the works council on a subject under co-determination means that the matter goes to arbitration – with the possibility of a binding award which may not only be in favour of the works council but also 'impractical' and 'legalistic' – employers tend to prefer whenever possible an internal negotiated solution. More importantly, the law gives works councils numerous opportunities to delay and obstruct managerial decisions by excessive insistence on legal formalities. Moreover, works councils frequently combine different subjects into 'packages', making their attitude on matters under co-determination conditional upon concessions of the employer on other matters. Both strategies, that of 'excessive legalism' as well as that of 'package dealing', involve a considerable stretching of the law and sometimes become, strictly speaking, illegal. For this reason, they require much legal expertise and political skill. To the extent that works councils know how to exploit their legal powers, refusing to make concessions may be extremely costly for employers. Especially in larger establishments, managements therefore have a strong interest in building up and maintaining a good working relationship with the works council. The price of this may be, and frequently is, a considerable *de facto* or even *de jure* (by works agreement) extension of the work council's legal information, consultation and co-determination rights.

Union attitudes toward the works constitution
German trade unions have always regarded the works constitution with mixed feelings. This is true particularly of the more radical wing of the

movement. While today the criticism is much more muted than it was in the 1920s, nevertheless there remains an important undercurrent of opposition. For many trade unionists, the legal establishment of a system of interest representation at the workplace which is independent of the unions still appears as an attempt by the State to create 'yellow' 'house unions'. From their perspective, the statutory representation system is a competitor to the unions set up to contain union influence at the workplace and thereby to weaken the union movement. The real function of the legal privileges of works councils is, in this view, to provide the works councils with a competitive advantage over workplace trade unions and to enable them to carry out what would otherwise be union functions.

No doubt, there is something in this. To the extent that workplace-related problems and conflicts are regulated in a non-union framework and without direct union involvement, the chances of trade unions being able to develop an independent power base within the plant are limited. On the other hand, while the institutions of the works constitution limit the role of the unions at the workplace, they are as institutions, open to union influence. Unions, like any other group of workers, are permitted to put up candidates for works council elections, and they have in fact done so in spite of their reservations on the statutory system. The reason is that works councils, despite the restrictions to which they are subject, are not merely consultative bodies but also have significant legal co-determination rights. Especially since the second world war, these rights have been extended several times by legislation. The more powerful and functionally important the works councils became as representatives of workers' interests, however, the less the unions could afford to leave them to non-union groups. Also, works councils are entitled under the law to considerable resources – such as office space, release from work, and clerical assistance – which would be very difficult to obtain for a voluntary union workplace organisation, especially in competition with an already existing works council system. In these conditions, it was almost inevitable that the unions at the workplace were pulled increasingly into the statutory system – or, to put it the other way around, that the latter was increasingly taken over by the unions. Today, more than 80 per cent of all works councillors are elected on the lists of DGB-affiliated industrial unions, and in the manufacturing industry and in the larger plants the percentage is still higher.

Whatever the legal distinctions between works councils and workplace union organisations may be, therefore – and whatever the remaining reservations of unions regarding the works constitution – the result of decades of practical experience is that the statutory institutions and the trade union organisations at the workplace today are functionally merged with each other. When trade union workplace organisations nominate their candidates for works council elections, they choose their most competent and influential members. As a result, the works council and the leadership of the union at the workplace usually consist of the same persons, and the workplace-related interests of workers are represented by the workplace union leaders in their capacity as works councillors. In this way, the statutory rights of works councils are turned *de facto* into trade union rights. How far this mutual incorporation has gone is reflected by the fact that most workers identify the works council with the union and *vice versa* – which is formally incorrect but *de facto* in many important respects true. The typical pattern for German unions in representing the interests of their members at the workplace is to act through the works councils system, using the works council, in a phrase often used by German trade union officials, as 'the extended arm of the union'.

Problems of control

The fact that most works councillors are trade union members does not by itself resolve the tensions between unions and works councils. However they may be composed, works councils still retain their legal independence. As works councillors are elected by the entire workforce – and may have to compete with non-union candidates – they may also develop a political power base of their own which the union may have to respect. For both reasons, unions cannot directly order works councils to follow a certain policy. To the extent that union control over works councils is in this sense limited, the works constitution may appear, as it does to many radical trade unionists, to support separatist 'syndicalist' tendencies at the workplace and thus contribute to undermining trade union solidarity.

However, there is reason to believe that this analysis is excessively legalistic. Given the *de facto* merger of the works council system with the workplace trade union, efforts of works councils to emphasise their independence from the unions appear rather as a special case of the separatist tendencies of workplace unions in general *vis-à-vis* external, territorial union structures. That such tendencies do indeed exist can be observed nowhere better than in Britain. Nevertheless, the legal independence of works councils makes it essential for unions to find ways of influencing works council policies. Formal rules, whether it is the law or the constitution of the union, cannot be of much help in this respect. Since the union is legally not a part of the statutory representation system, its influence on the works councils cannot be based on the law. Also, since works councils are not formally union bodies, their obligations towards the union cannot in principle be regulated by the union constitution. As a consequence, union control over works councils is always precarious and can be established only within a complex and mostly informal relationship of power and exchange. In the following, one specific strategy of the German trade unions to strengthen their political influence over works councils in the 1950s and 1960s will be discussed. While this strategy has enjoyed considerable publicity, it has not quite lived up to the expectations of the unions. In fact, its most interesting aspects are the way it failed and the consequences of this failure.

In the late 1950s, the IGM began a nation-wide campaign to revive the institution of *Vertrauensleute* or union stewards. *Vertrauensleute* are directly elected representatives of small groups of union members at the workplace. In the metal-working industry, they existed long before the creation of the statutory representation system and the formation of a centralised industrial union. Originally, the *Vertrauensleute* performed similar functions, and possessed similar powers, to British shop stewards. In fact, their role as shop floor representatives dates back to a time when unions did not exist at all, and the newly founded *Metallarbeiterverband* had considerable difficulties before the turn of the century in persuading the *Vertrauensleute* to co-operate with it.

The revival of the union stewards tradition in the 1950s was deliberately aimed by the IGM leadership at creating a 'countervailing force' against the works councils. Apart from being more numerous than works councillors, unions stewards are genuine union officials who are not subject to the restrictions of the works constitution. Unlike the works council, the body of union stewards in a plant (*Vertrauenskörper*) formally belongs to the voluntary system of interest representation and is an integral part of the union organisation. This makes it possible for union stewards to serve functions on behalf of the union which works councils are, at least formally, unable to fulfil. For instance, one function of the union stewards system was to broaden the influence of the union at the workplace beyond the limited number of works councillors and to contribute to the vital tasks of recruitment, dues collection, communication, social integration of members and mobilisation which had in the past been performed by the union's members on the works councils and, with declining successs, by the local branches. In addition, *Vertrauenskörper* were seen by many union officers, especially on the left wing of the movement, as possible instruments in the hands of the external union by which pressure could be applied to independent works councils. For this purpose, union stewards were granted the right by the union to elect their own leadership at plant level, and the full body of union stewards was given a strong role in the nomination of the candidates of the union at works council elections.

On the surface, the IGM *Vertrauensleute* strategy was quite successful. Throughout the 1960s and 1970s, the number of union stewards increased. In 1976, it was more than twice as high as in 1960 (Table 3.1). At the same time, the ratio of stewards over members improved by 67 per cent (Table 3.1). In 1976, there was about one steward to every 20 members; in 1960, the ratio had been one to 35. The number of plants with *Vertrauensleute* increased between 1960 and 1976 from 3,339 to 6,015. These plants employed about three quarters of all the workers in the industry. While in 1960 only about one half of the *Vertrauensleute* plants had an elected *Vertrauensleute* leadership, in 1976 this proportion had increased to 77 per cent (4,642 plants).

While these figures look impressive, the political success of the *Vertrauensleute* strategy was on the whole limited. In part this was due to organisational problems. Since *Vertrauenskörper* are not recognised by the works constitution and enjoy no legal privileges, they can as a rule be set up and maintained only under favourable conditions. Although, in 1976 the IGM had union stewards in 6,015 plants, the number of plants under IGM jurisdiction in that year which had works councils was 10,617. These plants employed about 94 per cent of the metal-working industry's total workforce. Thus, in more than 40 per cent of the plants in which an organised interest representation of workers existed, there were only works councillors and no union stewards. Since union stewards can become a significant political and organisational factor only when they have an elected leadership, the relationship between works councils and *Vertrauensleute* is even less favourable to the latter.

Another reason why the *Vertrauensleute* strategy did not quite fulfil

Table 3.1　*IGM Union Stewards in the Metalworking Industry*

Year	Number of union stewards	Union stewards per 10,000 employees		Union stewards per 10,000 members	
		Total	In plants with stewards	Total	In plants with stewards
1960	53,273	141	160	289	343
1962	66,814	159	189	351	414
1964	79,520	188	261	411	533
1967	88,001	217	281	449	593
1970	103,407	221	299	465	646
1973	123,595	264	344	495	670
1976	124,490	(278)	376	482	663

NB. Figures in brackets may be subject to statistical error
Source: IGM Head Office, Results of Union Steward Elections

the expectations of the leadership was the inevitable limitations in the stewards' political role. Regardless of whether or not a *Vertrauenskörper* exists in a plant, the representation of workplace-related interests *vis-à-vis* the employer remains a matter of co-determination and is thus firmly in the hands of the works council. Moreover, since collective bargaining in Germany is centralised at the industrial level, union stewards unlike British shop stewards have no opportunity to negotiate directly on behalf of their members. While they may be given a chance to participate in both co-determination and collective bargaining, this participation is always limited to advising others who make the final decisions. In this way, squeezed between the works council and the external union, and deprived of any actual responsibility, *Vertrauenskörper* frequently tended to adopt radical, ideological positions and, in particular, to engage in political warfare with the works council or the district officials. The more intensive these conflicts became, the more the unionised works councillors began to demand that the union draw a line and protect them from being interfered with by excessively ambitious *Vertrauensleute*. For the union, this often amounted to having to choose between the loyalty, however limited, of its works councillors and the full realisation of its original *Vertrauensleute* concept. Given the legal privileges of the works councils as the representatives of the day-to-day interests of the workforce – and the resulting impossibility of by-passing co-determination by workplace-based collective bargaining – this choice usually went in favour of the works councillors at the expense of the stewards.

In many ways, the actual results of the *Vertrauensleute* strategy, apart from a few notable exceptions, turned out to be the opposite of what had been intended. Rather than the stewards controlling the works councils, it usually was the works councils which took control of the stewards – if only to be able to ensure their own renomination at the next works council election. Frequently, the chairman of the works council, or another works council member, was also elected chairman of the *Vertrauenskörper*. In other plants, works councillors were formally co-opted on to the stewards' executive committee to ensure that the activities of the two bodies were 'properly co-ordinated'. One reason why works councils were able in these and other ways to re-establish gradually their hegemony over the union organisation at the workplace was their superior material resources. Another was, in quite a few cases, the active support of the full time district officers whose problems in controlling the stewards are considerably reduced when the stewards are already controlled by the works councils. The typical pattern in most plants with union stewards, as it evolved during the 1960s and 1970s, was not a dualism between union stewards and works council but a hierarchical subordination of the former to the latter.

While there may be exceptions, today *Vertrauenskörper* do not represent the political viewpoint of the union *vis-à-vis* the works council but, in a euphemistic formulation taken from the IGM rulebook, 'support the works council in its tasks'.

The organisational functions of the statutory representation system

The failure of the *Vertrauensleute* strategy was accompanied by a reinforcement of the dominant position of the works councils in the union workplace organisation. This development can be understood only if the organisational functions served by the institutions of the works constitution are taken into account. These functions are now briefly outlined.

First, the works council system provides for the horizontal integration of interest representation at the workplace and thus contributes to the establishment of representational monopolies of industrial unions. Works councils exercise their co-determination rights as unitary bodies on behalf of the workforce as a whole. Thus, they have to work out internal compromises between the different group interests among their constituents – blue-collar and white-collar workers, or skilled and unskilled workers – and to develop general interest definitions which can be shared by all or most sections of the workforce. The problems they face in this respect are in principle the same as those confronting industrial unions. By solving them with the assistance of the statutory framework of co-determination at the plant level, works councils relieve the political process of the voluntary industrial union of potentially divisive issues and conflicts. From the perspective of the internal politics of industrial unions, the horizontal integration of diverse sectional interests produced by the works councils represents a kind of 'intermediate product' upon which the union can draw in developing its even more general, industry-wide interest definition.

Another way in which the works constitution prevents union fragmentation is through the system of works council elections. Since works councils are unitary bodies, sectional interest unions have to compete for seats on them with industrial unions who try to appeal equally to all groups in the workforce. While the prospects of a sectional union becoming more than a small minority group on a works council are slim, industrial unions always stand a good chance of gaining more than half of the seats. As works councils usually decide by majority vote, a union with a majority of the seats can, at least in principle, turn the works council into its 'extended arm' and use the statutory co-determination rights as instruments of its policy. Obviously, this provides a strong incentive for heterogeneous groups to form coalitions broad enough to win an electoral majority.

The strategic pressures for the horizontal integration of union organisation are further reinforced by a strong 'incumbency effect' inherent in the works council system. Because of the unitary structure of works councils, it is usually only the majority union which can take advantage of the (latent) union security functions of the statutory system. Small sectional unions which occupy only a minor fraction of the seats on the works council can easily be excluded by their larger competitor from the system's organisational benefits. Since the majority union has a variety of opportunities to exploit the works council's legal co-determination rights for its own organisational purposes, the system gives non-sectional unions with a broad and heterogeneous constituency a significant competitive advantage. As a result, unions which have at one time gained a majority on a works council are likely to have more organisational advantages than their competitors, and the chances are that they will improve their position on the works council still further in successive elections. In this sense, the statutory system works in favour of a gradual growth of (unitary) industrial unionism at the expense of (fragmented) special interest unionism.

Second, in a country in which any form of compulsory union membership is illegal, the works council system has become over the years an important (latent) mechanism of union security. Works councillors are not permitted to use their office to do union business or to give organisational assistance to a union. In practice, however, this rule is hardly enforceable. For one thing, most works councillors are also union officers – which they can be under Section 74,3 of the Works Constitution Act of 1972. While, strictly speaking, their union role should be carried on only outside their office, this distinction is impossible to make on a wide range of subjects. Secondly, although an employer may in certain instances be able to establish that a works councillor has used his office for union purposes, he may be hesitant to take him to the Labour Court for this. Especially where works councils are politically strong and experienced, employers in the interest of good industrial relations usually prefer to look the other way rather than insist on a rigid enforcement of the law.

One way in which works councils perform union security functions is by representing the (majority) union's organisational interests *vis-à-vus* the employer. Employers dependent upon their works councils taking a 'co-operative' and 'reasonable' attitude in exercising co-determination rights are generally prepared to recognise their special relationship with the union. A widespread expression of this is the tacit understanding between employers and works councils that job applicants, at least in certain grades, will be accepted by the employer only if they are union members or if they agree to join the union. Usually, such surreptitious union-shop arrangements are implemented through the legal right of the works council to co-determination on the employment of new workers (Section 99,1 of the Works Constitution Act). Co-determination here means that the works council may on certain legal grounds raise objections to new employment in general, or to individual applicants, and employers are bound to take note of the objections (Section 99,2). In order to exercise this right works councils are entitled to an interview with job applicants. The fact that an applicant is not, or does not want to become, a union member is of course not among the reasons for which works councils can object to his or her employment. However, there is nothing in the law which forces an employer to explore whether the objections raised by the works council against a particular applicant are being used simply as a pretext, or whether the applicant has – illegally – been made to sign a union membership form during the interview with the works council.

Third, the statutory system of interest representation at the workplace supports the centralisation of union organisation and collective bargaining. In particular, it makes it possible for the external union to defend its 'strike monopoly' against forces at the workplace which may want to act on their own. While the statutory system supports some of the centrifugal tendencies of workplace organisations, it restricts others that could be particularly disruptive for industrial unions. To the extent that the union at the workplace is functionally merged into the statutory system, the legal obligation on works councils to respect existing industrial agreements (Section 2,1 of the Act) assists the external union in making centrally negotiated compromises binding on its workplace representatives. In this way, the primacy of industrial over workplace bargaining is extended into, and replicated within, the union organisation. Similarly, the general prohibition on works councils calling strikes (Section 74,2 of the Act) adds to the 'voluntary' means of control available to industrial unions in preventing autonomous action by individual workplace organisations. The same effect is brought about by the Act making the enforcement and supervision of industrial agreements a matter of co-determination rather than of workplace-based collective bargaining. As a result, disputes on the application of collective agreements go automatically to conciliation and arbitration and cannot become the subject of workplace industrial action. Thus, strikes remain limited to the level of the industry as a whole, and the control of the 'strike weapon' remains in the hands of the central union leadership.

Fourth, the statutory representation system allows for supplementary bargaining at the workplace without adverse consequences for the stability of the industry-wide bargaining system. It thus contributes to the solution of one of the most difficult problems of any system of central regulation of wages and working conditions. Industrial agreements apply equally to all firms in an industry but the structural and economic characteristics of individual firms, of course, vary widely. Regulatory mechanisms failing to take such differences into account run the risk of becoming meaningless. For example, during economic booms industrial agreements do not exhaust the ability to pay of those firms which are benefiting from the economic upturn. As a result of pressure either from the market or from the workforce, actual wages in these firms may considerably exceed official wage rates. The wider the 'wage drift', however, the less relevant are the industry-wide negotiations for the individual workplace, and the less realistic is centrally co-ordinated, 'solidaristic' union strategy. An example of an originally centralised bargaining system which disintegrated as a consequence of wage drift is, of course, the British one.

Trying to impose uniform regulations on a heterogeneous industrial reality may lead not to uniformity but to disintegration and fragmentation. General rules can be successfully enforced in different situations only when they are flexible enough to be modified according to circumstances. Industrial agreements, for example, have to be corrected in favour of workers in firms which are above-average in profitability in order to be acceptable to those workers. Otherwise, such workers would prefer to go for separate, company or shop-floor agreements. On the other hand, too much flexibility renders general regulations ineffective and also gives rise to fragmentation. The problem for industry-wide bargaining systems, therefore, is to have a correction mechanism at the level of the individual firm which is strong enough to make the central agreement generally acceptable, and weak enough not to render it, as in Britain, meaningless. In Germany the functions of such a mechanism are successfully performed by the statutory representation system.

A special problem German unions have with wage drift concerns the legal status of payments made in excess of industrial agreements. As such payments are not laid down in a collective contract, they are legally voluntary and can in principle be withdrawn by the employer at any time. To prevent this, and to improve the control of the collective bargaining system over the growing wage drift generally, German unions in the 1950s began to consider the possibility of inserting so-called 'opening clauses' (*Öffnungsklauseln*) into industrial agreements. Under the Collective Agreements Act (*Tarifvertragsgesetz*), such clauses permit unions to open, following the conclusion of an industrial agreement, a 'second wage round' in individual, particularly prosperous firms, with the aim of gaining supplementary agreements on additional increases in line with these firms' above-average ability to pay. However, this approach never became official policy. The primary reason was not the expected heavy resistance of the employers but rather resistance within the unions themselves. The main argument of the opponents was that opening clauses, by giving individual workplace unions the right to collective bargaining and inevitably the right to strike, would undermine organisational unity and solidarity at the industrial level. It was felt that there was a strong possibility that the workforce of large, economically strong firms would be unwilling to go on strike for the industrial agreement because they would know that the size of their wage increase would be settled only in the 'second round' of negotiations. If workers in strong bargaining positions saved their 'strike power' for themselves, industrial settlements would become lower and less meaningful, and the redistribution of bargaining power between different groups of workers on which industrial unionism depends would no longer be possible. It was because of such considerations that no union ever made an attempt to get an opening clause inserted into an industrial agreement.

This is not to say that there are no 'second round' wage negotiations in German firms. The point is, however, that these are not conducted within the framework of collective bargaining but, strangely enough, within that of co-determination. Since industrial agreements are legally binding on the union as a whole, demands in firms with above-average economic performance for additional increases on top of the general increase cannot, in the absence of opening clauses, be officially raised by workplace union representatives. Thus, they are taken up unofficially by the same persons in their capacity as works councillors. To get employers to negotiate with them over wages, works councils informally link their wage demands with subjects under co-determination. Since it is illegal for works councils to negotiate over wages, talks between works councils and employers on supplementary pay increases cannot lead to a collective agreement but only to an informal understanding on a formally unilateral pay raise by the employer. At the most, pay bargaining between works councils and employers can be disguised as co-determination on the 'application' of the industrial agreement, especially of its clauses on piece rates. To the extent that this is possible, supplementary bargaining may result in a works agreement.

As far as the car industry is concerned, the informal opportunities for supplementary pay bargaining provided by the statutory representation system go a long way in accounting for the industry's integration into the collective bargaining machinery for the engineering industry. Since the ability to pay of firms in the car industry tends to be higher than in the engineering industry generally, there are in principle good reasons for a separate car industry agreement, and there are forces within the IGM pressing in this direction. One major reason why such forces have up to now not prevailed is that the deficiencies of the industrial agreement from the perspective of car workers can be compensated in the unofficial 'second wage round' at the level of individual plants. Since the special interests of car workers, as distinct from the interests of metalworkers in general, can in this way be taken care of below the level of the car industry as a whole, most of the arguments in favour of an industrial agreement for the car industry are pre-empted. The same holds, for the same reasons, for a special car industry trade group within IGM. In this sense, the statutory representation system assists the IGM in keeping up its unitary organisational structure in the face of considerable internal heterogeneity.

Union workplace organisation in the car industry

In 1975, 509 of the above 830 plants which belonged to the car industry had works councils. These plants employed 96.2 per cent of the car industry's workforce, and 71.5 per cent of their employees were organised in the IGM (Table 3.2). While the number of plants which had works councils seems to have increased between the mid-1960s and the mid-1970s by about 10 per cent the proportion of the workforce represented by works councils was always higher than 93 per cent and was thus well above the average for the metalworking industry.

The IGM does not publish the results of works council elections by industries, and it is therefore not possible to provide information on the number of works councillors in the car industry and the percentage of

Table 3.2   Works Councils in Car Industry Plants

Year	Number of plants with works councils	As per cent of all plants	Number of employees in plants with works councils (000s)	As per cent of all employees	IGM density ratio
1961	(288)	. . .	373.7	93.6	56.8
1963	(284)	(29.7)(a)	434.5	93.8	51.1
1965	438	51.0	523.8	(101.2)	49.8
1968	423	. . .	550.1	(99.9)	51.0
1972	517	60.6(b)	569.1	93.5	64.6
1975	509	61.5(c)	544.6	96.2	71.5

(a) 1962 figure

(b) 1971 figure

(c) 1974 figure

. . . Not available

NB. Figures in brackets may be affected by statistical error

Source: IGM Head Office, Results of Works Council Elections

IGM members among them. The main reason why IGM does not publish industry-specific election results is that it is anxious to hide its 'weak spots' in industries like electrical engineering. Poor performance in certain industries could give rise to demands for special organisational efforts and for industry-specific organisational structures which may later develop tendencies to turn into trade groups. This, however, might weaken the union's internal cohesion, and it would be incompatible with the IGM's present unitary structure. Works council election results for two major car manufacturing firms are, however, given in Chapters 6 and 7.

Throughout the period of observation, the number of plants in the car industry with *Vertrauensleute*, and their percentage in relation to all plants in the industry, was considerably below that of plants with works councils. For instance, while in 1976 union stewards were elected in 300 car industry plants (Table 3.3), one year earlier works councils had been elected in 509 plants (Table 3.2). However, except for the early 1960s, the percentage of the industry's total workforce employed in *Vertrauensleute* plants was only slightly lower than the respective percentage for the works council plants, indicating that the plants which had works councils but no union stewards were very small and thus of little political importance. The density of IGM membership in the two

Table 3.3   *IGM Union Stewards in Car Industry Plants*

Year	Number of plants with union stewards	As per cent of all plants	Number of employees in plants with union stewards (000s)	As per cent of all employees	IGM density ratio
1962	(165)	(17.2)	379.2	82.0	. . .
1964	(287)	(33.4)(a)	476.7	95.0	50.0
1967	332	. . .	489.7	. . .	52.7
1970	362	42.4(b)	640.4	. . .	56.0
1973	350	42.3(c)	577.3	91.4	68.7
1976	308	. . .	513.2	. . .	72.8

(a) 1965 figure
(b) 1971 figure
(c) 1974 figure
. . . Not available
NB. Figures in brackets may be affected by statistical error
Source: IGM Head Office, Results of Works Council Elections

categories of plants was almost identical.

As to the relative size of the IGM workplace organisation, 4.4 per cent or every twenty-third member of the IGM in car industry plants with *Vertrauensleute*, and 4.8 per cent of the total IGM membership, held an office as union steward in 1976 (Table 3.4). The proportion of all IGM members in 1975 who were works councillors was 2.3 per cent. In comparing the number of works councillors and union stewards, allowance has to be made for overlapping membership. Since by the mid-1970s about a quarter of the *Vertrauensleute* in the metalworking industry also sat on works councils, the number of those who were *Vertrauensleute* only was below 200 per 10,000 employees in the metalworking industry. Of all IGM workplace representatives, about 40 per cent were works councillors and 60 per cent, *Vertrauensleute*; about half of the works councillors (18 per cent of the total) in addition had the status of union steward. Comparable data for the car industry is not available. Nevertheless, the figures support the generalisation that

Table 3.4   Works Council Members and IGM Union Stewards in the Metal-working and Car Industries

Year	Works council members per 10,000 employees A	Works council members per 10,000 IGM members A	IGM union stewards per 10,000 employees A	IGM union stewards per 10,000 employees B	IGM union stewards per 10,000 IGM members A	IGM union stewards per 10,000 IGM members B
1961	115	213	...	...	...	...
1962	...	...	159	153	351	...
1963	125	227	...	...	...	...
1964	...	...	188	198	411	417
1965	124	224	...	...	...	...
1967	...	...	217	230	449	429
1968	127	223	...	...	...	...
1970	...	...	221	246	465	427
1972	144	226	...	...	...	...
1973	...	...	264	269	494	429
1975	163	226	...	...	...	...
1976	...	...	...	...	482	442

A – Metalworking industry as a whole
B – Car industry
Note: Works council members per 10,000 IGM members includes only those works council members who are members of the IGM. Union stewards per 10,000 IGM members in the car industry includes only those IGM members who work in plants with union stewards
Source: IGM Head Office, Results of Works Council Elections, Results of Union Steward Elections

contrary to widespread assumptions, the union stewards system does not involve many more union members than the statutory representation system, and that even in quantitative terms it has failed to establish itself clearly as the leading element within the union workplace organisation.

Footnotes

[1] The historical origins of the works councils system go back to the *Vaterländisches Hilfsdienstgesetz* of 1916. After the first world war unions and employers associations reached an understanding on the introduction by legislation of a general Works Constitution of which works councils were to form the core element. In effect, the new legislation amounted to an amalgamation of the participation schemes of the war economy with the revolutionary workers movement that had sprung up after the war in all parts of the country. In 1933, the works councils were abolished by the Nazis. Immediately after the end of the Nazi regime, works councils in many places re-emerged spontaneously and, in the absence of the owners, organised the resistance against the dismantling of industrial plants by the Allies. Sometimes they even took over the management of their establishments. The new Federal Republic reinstituted the works councils as representatives of the workers in the Works Constitution Act of 1952. While there were many changes in detail, the Act on the whole followed the pattern of the Works Constitution of the Weimar Republic. Twenty years later, it was replaced by the Works Constitution Act of 1972 by which the system was further elaborated and adapted to recent economic, technical and political changes.

[2] There are two different kinds of co-determination in Germany: co-determination at the plant level (*betriebliche Mitbestimmung*) which is exercised through the works council, and co-determination at the enterprise level (*Mitbestimmung auf Unternehmensebene*) which is exercised through workers representatives on the supervisory board. While the first type of co-determination exists in all establishments with more than four employees, the latter is limited to large companies. Although it could be argued that *betriebliche Mitbestimmung* is more important in practice than supervisory board *Mitbestimmung*, the latter usually attracts more public attention – so much so that the term '*Mitbestimmung*' is often used to refer exclusively to the supervisory board type. Details on co-determination at the enterprise level will be given in Chapter 4.

[3] The term Labour Court is a literal translation of the German *Arbeitsgericht* but a more appropriate term might be industrial relations court. Unions and employers play an important role in the operation of the Labour Court system. Labour Courts consist of one professional judge, one employers' representative and one union representative.

4 The Structure of Industrial Relations at Volkswagen

The origins of Volkswagen go back to the period of the Nazi regime. Production in what is now Wolfsburg began in the summer of 1938. The owner of the company at this time was a suborganisation of the Deutsche Arbeitsfront (German Labour Front) which was the fascist successor to the former labour unions. One aim of the founders of Volkswagen was to promote mass car ownership as a way of satisfying aspirations of workers for a higher standard of living (Volkswagen literally translated means 'peoples' car'). In fact, the organisation which nominally controlled Volkswagen then was called *Kraft durch Freude* (Strength Through Joy) and was one of the main instruments of Nazi social policy. Its original mission was to promote government-controlled mass tourism on a large scale and to organise other recreational activities such as summer camps or sports events. A second, equally important function of Volkswagen was, of course, to provide motor transport for the German army, and it was exclusively this purpose which the company served from 1939 until the end of the war.

The first Volkswagen plant was set up on a greenfield site in a rural area 200 kilometres west of Berlin, close to one of the main autobahnen and next to one of the main arteries of the German canal system (Mittellandkanal). The settlement built to accommodate workers from other parts of the country – the majority of the workforce continued to live in their villages nearby – was called Kraft-durch-Freude City. It was only after the war that the name was changed to Wolfsburg. However, the place remained a company town into the 1950s and 1960s, with Volkswagen being the only major employer and with all land being owned by the company. Production methods were highly advanced from the beginning, as much of the equipment and the technical know-how were bought from Ford in Detroit. (Henry Ford was decorated for this by Hitler in 1938). After the war, Wolfsburg was in the British Zone and Volkswagen came under British control for a short while. In 1949, the company was handed over to the government of the newly founded Federal Republic.

The postwar expansion of Volkswagen began in 1948, immediately after production resumed. For almost 20 years, the company produced only two models, the Beetle and a transport van, the main components of which, such as the engine, were identical. Although the Beetle was slightly changed almost every year, it continued to be based in its main technical characteristics on the prewar model designed by Ferdinand Porsche. During the 1950s and especially the 1960s, the company set up new plants in Germany and abroad. By the mid-1970s, it had establishments in Wolfsburg, Hannover, Kassel, Emden, Salzgitter and Braunschweig as well as in Brazil, Mexico, South Africa, Belgium and Nigeria. All of these plants were newly constructed. Also, in the late 1960s Volkswagen acquired, little by little, the Audi NSU car manufacturing company. The main plants of Audi NSU are in Ingolstadt and Neckarsulm which unlike the Volkswagen plants are located in Southern Germany. The headquarters of the company and its main establishment remained at Wolfsburg and unless otherwise indicated it is with the Wolfsburg plant that the following account will be concerned.

Volkswagen as a company: the structure of control

As with all joint stock companies in Germany, Volkswagen has a two-tier board structure. The basic functions of the supervisory board on the one hand and the management board on the other are regulated by statute. While individual companies have the freedom to introduce some modifications, in principle all German companies are organised in an identical way. Thus, the supervisory board at Volkswagen as well as elsewhere consists of elected representatives of the shareholders and, under co-determination, of the workforce, whereas the management board consists of professional managers. Although the supervisory board appoints the members of the management board and formulates general policy, it must not interfere with the day-to-day management of the company. This is exclusively the concern of the management board.

The size of both the supervisory and the management board depends on the size of the company. At Volkswagen in 1975,[1] the supervisory board had 21 members while the management board consisted of 9 members. Audi NSU still has its own supervisory board on which the shareholders' representatives are all appointed by the Volkswagen management board. Audi NSU also has its own management board.

While the basic structure of the Volkswagen board system is, for legal reasons, the same as in other German companies, the composition of the two boards was, and still is, different from other companies in a number of ways mainly because the the the company's origins. For a period after the war, Volkswagen was in public ownership. Since public ownership of manufacturing companies was in conflict with the philosophy of the then conservative Federal Government, throughout the 1950s the government looked for a politically acceptable way to return the company to private ownership. In the early 1960s three-fifths of the Volkswagen capital was sold in small shares and limited numbers as

Volksaktien (people's shares) to private owners. Twenty per cent of the capital was kept by the Federal Republic, another fifteen remained with the *Land* of Lower Saxony (Niedersachsen). The remaining five per cent is held by Volkswagen Foundation which, like the Ford Foundation, supports various cultural activities.

Like all big companies outside the coal and steel industry, Volkswagen since 1952 has been under a limited kind of economic co-determination. Co-determination rights of workers in German industry are institutionalised at two levels: at the plant level where they are exercised by the works council, and at the company level ('economic co-determination') where they are exercised by workers' representatives on the boards. Economic co-determination exists in two different versions depending on what industry a company belongs to. Full economic co-determination as it exists in the coal and steel industry involves an equal number of shareholders and workers' representatives on the supervisory board (parity). In addition, one member of the management board – who is in charge of the personnel and manpower department (*Arbeitsdirektor*) – cannot be appointed by the supervisory board without the consent of the workers' representatives on the board. By contrast, under the limited version of economic co-determination as it applied to the rest of German industry until 1976, workers' representatives held only one-third of the seats on the supervisory board, and the law did not provide for an *Arbeitsdirektor* at the management board level. In 1976, the Social-Liberal government passed a new statute on economic co-determination outside coal and steel to increase the number of workers' representatives to one below parity (one member has to be a representative of the middle management; in case of a deadlock the chairman, who always comes from the shareholders' side, has a casting vote) and made it obligatory for each company above a certain size to have an *Arbeitsdirektor*. The 1976 statute, however, does not provide for a special appointment procedure so that the *Arbeitsdirektor* can be appointed like all other members of the management board by majority vote of the supervisory board.

Under the statute in force in 1975, of the 21 Volkswagen supervisory board members 14 came from the shareholders while 7 were representatives of the workers. The representatives of the shareholders are elected by the annual general meeting. Because of the wide dispersion of the Volksaktien, the Federal Government and the Land of Lower Saxony are by far the largest single shareholders. General meetings are dominated by them together with the banks which under German law are entitled to vote on behalf of the shares they have in deposit. This is reflected in the composition of the shareholders' side of the supervisory board. Two of the 14 representatives in 1975 came from the Federal government; they were the permanent secretaries of the departments of

Economics and Finance. Another two were from the Land government of Lower Saxony which had delegated its Finance and Economics ministers. Of the remaining 10, no less than four were executives of banking companies, two came from big supplier firms, one represented the Volkswagen dealers, and only two represented the small shareholders. The remaining member, the chairman, did not belong to any of these groups. Until mid-1975, the supervisory board was chaired by a retired permanent secretary of the Defence department. In the course of the events which will be described in Chapter 5, a new chairman was appointed who was the managing director of Salzgitter AG, a big manufacturing concern owned by the Federal government.

A characteristic aspect of the composition of the shareholders side at Volkswagen is that one of the bank representatives in 1975 was the managing director of the Bank für Gemeinwirtschaft, Walter Hesselbach. The Bank für Gemeinwirtschaft is jointly owned by the DGB and its affiliated unions. In addition to handling the financial affairs of the unions – including in particular the administration of their strike funds – the Bank für Gemeinwirtschaft engages in normal banking activities and was in fact so successful that by the mid-1970s it was the fourth largest private bank in Germany. This explains why a trade unionist like Hesselbach could represent the shareholders on the Volkswagen supervisory board – the reason being that the unions' banking company represented a large number of small shareholders at the general meeting. Given his background, Hesselbach could, of course, as well have represented the workers – and indeed did serve as a workforce representative on a number of other company boards. What is more, since he was often consulted by the Chancellor as a personal adviser on economic matters, he might conceivably also have represented the Federal government. It appears that because of these simultaneous affiliations to all parties involved, and because of his high prestige with the unions, the banking community and the government alike, Hesselbach was able to play a crucial role in solving the management crisis at Volkswagen in 1975 and again in 1978 (see Chapters 5–7).

On the union side, there were seven workers' representatives on the supervisory board in 1975. By law, workers' representatives have to be elected every three years by the workforce. Just as in works council elections, all employees, regardless of union membership, are eligible to vote. Candidates can be nominated by unions or any other group of employees. Before the 1976 amendment, the right to stand for election was not dependent on whether a candidate was employed with the company. The only legal requirement was that he had the support of a minimum number of voters. This provision was sometimes used by the unions to place full time officials as 'outside representatives' on supervisory boards of important companies. However, since union workplace organisations normally prefer to be represented by their own leaders, the number of outside representatives was never high. The situation is different under the coal and steel type of co-determination where a certain proportion of the seats on the workers' side are by statute reserved for external representatives who do not need to be elected but can be directly appointed by the union. The 1976 extension of co-determination made a certain number of external workers' representatives mandatory but did not grant the unions the right of direct appointment. Under the new law, external representatives have to be elected in the same way as internal representatives, except that the votes for them are counted separately.

All seven workers' representatives on the Volkswagen supervisory board in 1975 were members of the IGM. Two of them came from Wolfsburg: Hermann Ehlers, the chairman of the Wolfsburg works council and the Volkswagen central works council, and another works council member. The others were the chairmen of the works councils of Kassel and Emden, the vice chairman of the Audi NSU works council, a white-collar employee from the Hannover plant and Eugen Loderer, the chairman of IGM in Frankfurt.

The presence of Loderer on the Volkswagen supervisory board demonstrates the importance attached by the IGM to Volkswagen. As a supervisory board member at Volkswagen, Loderer continued a tradition started by his predecessor as IGM chairman, Otto Brenner, who was also on the Volkswagen board.

During the Volkswagen crisis of the mid-1970s, the composition of the company's supervisory board became a matter of considerable public attention. Up to March 1976, both the Federal government and the government of Lower Saxony were Social-Liberal coalitions. (In March 1976, a Conservative-Liberal coalition took over in Lower Saxony). Because of the leading role of the SPD in the two governments and the close relationship between the SPD and the unions, it was often suspected that the four government delegates, if put under pressure by the IGM, would side with the union representatives against the other shareholders. Similar suspicions were held with regard to the managing director of the Bank für Gemeinwirtschaft who was perceived by the public much more as a unionist than as a representative of the shareholders. One of the points the conservative press used to make in the initial phase of the crisis was that, altogether, 12 out of the 21 members of the supervisory board were either works councillors, unionists, or delegates of governments closely allied with the union movement. In much of the public debate, these were treated as one block with a common interest and a common policy. To denote what they perceived as a situation in which 'the union side' had an effective majority on the supervisory board – instead of only one-third or even one half of the seats – the press and conservative politicians during the crisis invented the terms of 'over-co-determination' or 'over-parity'.

However invalid such charges may have been, there are indeed indications that the shareholders' side on the Volkswagen supervisory board was and is more accessible to the union than is usual, and that the union's informal position within the company is stronger than the formal one. Thus, Loderer just as Brenner before him, not only was a member of the supervisory board but also served as its vice chairman. While it is the rule in the coal and steel industry to appoint the leading workers' representative to this position, this was rare for the general, one-third type of co-determination that existed before 1976. Whether or not one of the vice-chairman positions goes to a representative of the workers is of more than symbolic importance – although the symbolic significance of a union leader chairing an annual general meeting in the absence of the supervisory board chairman must not be underestimated. Many decisions of supervisory boards are prepared and in fact often pre-empted by a small committee consisting of the chairman and the vice chairmen. (The other two vice chairmen of the Volkswagen board in 1975 were the permanent secretary of the Federal Finance department and the Finance Minister of Lower Saxony). There can be no doubt that its control over one of the vice chairman positions strengthened the union's institutional position in the power structure of the company.

Perhaps even more important was that Volkswagen, although not required by law to do so, conceded to the union an informal right to select its personnel director. In practice, Volkswagen thus has – as a result of an understanding between the shareholders and the union – an *Arbeitsdirektor* as if the company were subject to coal and steel co-determination. When a personnel director, who is one of the nine management board members each of which is in charge of a specific department, is appointed, the majority of the supervisory board wait for a recommendation by the workers' representatives. This it passes as a formal decision. As a result, the personnel and manpower division at Volkswagen is, in effect, under exactly the same kind of union control as in coal and steel. In 1975, the personnel director was Peter Frerk, a former head of the welfare department of the city of Hannover – the capital of Lower Saxony – and a Social Democrat. During the events which will be described in the following chapters, Frerk lost the confidence of the works council and of IGM headquarters and was removed from his post in late 1977 at the request of the workers' representatives on the supervisory board. His successor was a former IGM headquarters official who was at that time *Arbeitsdirektor* with Krupp in Essen. Although Frerk had to give up the personnel department, he remained on the executive board where he was put in charge of public relations.

Collective bargaining at Volkswagen

Collective bargaining arrangements at Volkswagen differ from the general pattern in German industry. While normally wages and conditions are regulated by industrial agreements covering all firms in a *Land* or in the entire country, Volkswagen has always had a company agreement. When after the war the company was under public ownership, it was not permitted to join an employers' association. Since industrial agreements negotiated by associations of employers are formally binding only on their members, IGM in the case of Volkswagen had to resort to company bargaining. No other major firm in the metalworking industry has a similar bargaining arrangement. Company bargaining at Volkswagen extends only to the Volkswagen plants and excludes Audi NSU which regardless of the merger remains in its regional employers' association and thus continues to be covered by the regional industrial agreement for Nord-Württemberg/Nord-Baden.

The bargaining machinery of the IGM at Volkswagen resembles that used for regional industrial negotiations. As in the metalworking industry as a whole, the IGM is the only union at Volkswagen with negotiating rights. The important bodies are a union pay committee consisting of about 60 representatives of the members from all Volkswagen plants, and a negotiating committee led by the regional secretary for Lower Saxony (most Volkswagen plants are located in this *Land*) and consisting of a small number of works council members and *Vertrauensleute* delegated by the pay committee. Just as in industrial negotiations, the regional secretary as the principal negotiator is subject to directions from the national executive. All decisions during the course of negotiations require authorisation by the national executive whose experts are closely involved in every stage of the process. The role of the pay committee is limited, again as in industrial negotiations, to advising the national executive on the attitudes of the members and to voting on decisions affecting the formal relations with the employer, such as termination of contracts, initial demands, calling a strike vote, going to arbitration, calling or ending a strike, and signing an agreement.

For IGM, company bargaining at Volkswagen has advantages as well as disadvantages. Company agreements preclude wage drift and put the union in control of the entire wage structure of all wage components. As this deprives the works council of an important opportunity to gain independence, the company agreement strengthens the position of the external union in relation to its workplace organisation.

On the other hand, while wage drift and surreptitious pay bargaining by the works council may have disadvantages for industrial unions, they also have important advantages. Since Volkswagen is a large company with an above-average ability to pay and a highly unionised workforce, wages at Volkswagen are bound to exceed those in most other firms in the metalworking industry. The same, of course, applies to the wages at other major car producers covered by regional industrial agreements. However, whereas in the latter case the industrial agreement can be corrected through a second wage round, this is not possible at Volkswagen where official wage rates and actual wages are identical. For this reason, the Volkswagen company agreement must exceed the general industrial agreement applying, say, to Opel Rüsselsheim. One of the problems this creates for IGM is that the media from time to time accuse the union of exploiting its strong position on the supervisory board and the management board at Volkswagen to extract unduly high wages. This theme was particularly prominent during the crisis of the mid-1970s when some commentators tried to put the blame on the IGM's allegedly 'excessive' wage policy. The answer of the union to allegations of this kind is that the correct comparison is between actual earnings and not official wage rates, and that in these terms there are no differences between Volkswagen and other big car producers. Whether or not this is actually true is difficult to decide; indications are that Volkswagen wages are in fact somewhat higher than Opel wages, although the difference is not dramatic.[2]

It is not just to fend off public criticism, however, that IGM denies so staunchly that there are any differences in pay between Volkswagen and other German car manufacturers. The other reason is that if such differences did in fact exist and members became aware of it, workplace organisations in car manufacturing companies other than Volkswagen would also want to have a company agreement or, alternatively, might ask for a special industrial agreement for the car industry. Too obvious disparities between the wages at Volkswagen and at the other car manufacturers would undermine the entire multi-industrial bargaining system, and with it the existence of IGM as an organisation. This is why IGM uses the company bargaining mechanism at Volkswagen only with great caution and it is for this reason that centralisation of decision-making and the controlling position of full time officers are so strictly defended by the national leadership even where bargaining is confined to only one company.

On the other hand, minimising the difference between the company agreement at Volkswagen and the regional industrial agreements may not necessarily be in the interest of Volkswagen workers. Just as workers in other firms may feel shortchanged if the Volkswagen agreement is higher than theirs, Volkswagen workers in the absence of opportunities for a second wage round may feel disadvantaged if their settlement is not higher than the industrial agreement. An example of how this conflict can in certain conditions impair the stability of the bargaining system is shown by the wage round of 1978. After all regions had settled successively in a few weeks at about five per cent, the regional secretary of Lower Saxony as the chief negotiator at Volkswagen asked the Volkswagen pay committee to approve a negotiated settlement of about the same size. In view of the ongoing Volkswagen boom at that time the pay committee rejected the proposal, and negotiations had to be resumed. When no progress was made, IGM headquarters followed a proposal by the pay committee and took a strike vote. Shortly before a strike was called the company gave in, and a settlement was reached providing for an increase of between 6–7 per cent. Although many Volkswagen workers believed that this was still too low, in the final vote the opposition was not strong enough for the settlement to be rejected. One day after the agreement was signed, an unofficial strike started at Opel in Rüsselsheim where dissatisfaction with the low regional agreement had been intense. Although the second wage round had already been completed, informal negotiations between the works council and the management had to be re-opened, and the settlement had again to be improved.

IGM membership at Volkswagen

Almost all of the manual workers at Volkswagen, and about two-thirds of the white-collar workers, are IGM members. While in the early 1950s IGM seems to have had some difficulties organising the blue-collar workforce at Wolfsburg, in the last one and a half decades whatever problems there may have been have disappeared. The situation is similar at the other German Volkswagen plants and at Audi NSU, except that the relative number of white-collar workers at Wolfsburg is higher than elsewhere so that the overall density ratio tends to be slightly lower.

A few exceptions notwithstanding, there are no members of other unions at Volkswagen. Workers who do not belong to IGM are as a rule unorganised. This applies in particular to the white-collar section of the workforce where the German staff union (DAG) has failed to gain any significant membership. Accordingly, no other union apart from IGM has negotiating rights at Volkswagen. Since workplace bargaining takes place in the legal form of co-determination by the works council, the question of recognition of further unions cannot arise.

While there is no formal closed shop at Volkswagen – and cannot be by law – there are effective informal and sublegal mechanisms ensuring that almost everybody who takes up employment with the company joins IGM. As in other big companies, the central role in this respect is played by the works council which is dominated by IGM members and which uses its co-determination rights concerning the employment of new workers as an instrument of union security. Candidates for employment are advised during their interview in the works council's office that all of their future work mates are organised with IGM and that the works council would welcome it if the new recruit would also join. Exceptions are made for certain higher categories of white-collar workers whose employment is deemed essential by the company and whose 'freedom not to be organised' the personnel department would therefore be prepared to defend if necessary. The failure of unions other than IGM to organise sizeable membership at Volkswagen is at least partly due to the dominant position of IGM on the works council which prevents competitors using the works council's co-determination rights for their organisational purposes.

Works council and Vertrauensleute

Works councils are elected every three years. The composition of the Wolfsburg works council after the 1978 election was basically the same as that of the works council elected in 1975. The number of employees eligible to vote in 1978 was 54,000. By law, this meant that 63 works councillors had to be elected. Since 18 per cent of the employees were white-collar workers, 12 of the works councillors had to come from this group. Eighty-five per cent of those eligible to vote took part in the election.

Among the blue-collar workforce, four groups including the IGM had put up lists of candidates; 76.6 per cent of the vote, and 40 of the 51 seats for blue-collar works councillors, went to the IGM. The second strongest list was that of the Christian Metal Workers Association (CMV) which got 16.7 per cent and 8 seats. The CMV is an affiliate of the Christian Union Federation (CGB) which nominally is in competition with the DGB but has only small pockets of membership and neither negotiating rights nor significant electoral support at works council elections; the relatively strong position of the CMV at Volkswagen is exceptional. Politically, the CMV like the other CGB affiliates is close to the right wing of the Christian Democratic Party (CDU); the left wing of the CDU supports the DGB and refuses to co-operate with the CGB. Another two seats, and 4.5 per cent of the blue-collar vote, went to the German Workers Association (DAV), an organisation which exists only at Volkswagen. Finally, one seat in the blue-collar group was won by an independent candidate.

Election results were similar among white-collar workers. Among the 9,816 employees eligible to vote in this group, voter turnout was 84.7 per cent. Sixty-six per cent of the voters supported the IGM list which accordingly received eight of the 12 white-collar seats; 29.5 per cent of the vote, and the remaining four seats, went to the list of the DAG (German Staff Union). The CMV in this group got only 4.4 per cent which was not enough to win a seat. All in all, taking blue-collar and white-collar workers together, the IGM received 72.7 per cent of the votes cast and won 48 of the 63 works council seats. Just as in the preceding years, the 1978 election thus gave the IGM a comfortable majority and enabled it to use the Volkswagen works council, within the legal restrictions applying to the statutory representation system, as an instrument of its policy.

Under the Works Constitution Act, the chairman and the vice chairman of the works council are elected from its ranks for three years by the new works council at its first meeting. Large works councils like those in the Volkswagen plants also elect a small standing committee which is responsible for conducting the council's day-to-day business. At Wolfsburg, the standing committee consists of nine members plus the chairman and the vice chairman. In addition, there is a formal division of tasks and responsibilities among works council members which is also determined by the full works council.

According to Section 38 of the Works Constitution Act, the minimum number of works council members to be released from their normal work duties in a plant of the size of Volkswagen in Wolfsburg is 38. The Act provides for the possibility of more far-reaching arrangements made 'by collective agreement or works agreement'. This has been made use of at Volkswagen where under a works agreement all works councillors without exception are released from factory work. The same works agreement stipulates that works council members, regardless of the job they had before they were elected, have white-collar status (so that they do not have to clock in and can leave the premises at any time) and get the salary of a foreman plus an allowance for 10 hours of overtime. (Works councillors who before their election have earned more than a foreman continue to get their previous pay). In 1977, a works councillor at Volkswagen thus had a minimum income before tax of DM 3,800 per month which was about one and a half times as much as the income of an average Volkswagen worker. This practice is unusual and has frequently met with criticism among the Wolfsburg workforce as well as within IGM.

Each works councillor at Volkswagen in Wolfsburg has his own office and telephone. Works council offices are spread all over the plant. While the offices of the leading works council members are located in the same building as the personnel department, works councillors responsible for single shops have their offices there. For every five or six works council members, there is one typist who, like the office space and the telephone, is provided under Section 40 of the Works Constitution Act by the company. The details of how the company discharges its obligations to the works council under this section are laid down in a works agreement.

Under the amended Works Constitution Act of 1972 the works councils of all six German Volkswagen plants form a central company works council. Whereas in many other large companies central works councils existed before they were prescribed by law, at Volkswagen the central works council was not set up until 1973 when it had become mandatory. All members of the central works council are organised in the IGM. The central works council is chaired by the leader of the Wolfsburg works council, Hermann Ehlers, who also serves as a workers' representative on the supervisory board.

As it includes among its members the chairmen and vice chairmen of all six local works councils, the central works council is one of the centres of power within the statutory representation system at Volkswagen. By law, central works councils have to limit their activities to matters which are either explicitly referred to them by one of the local works councils or which cannot be resolved by individual works councils at plant level. However, there are strong interests on the part of the leading works council members – who as a rule sit on the central works council – to increase the latter's responsibilities. By transferring contentious matters to the central works council, local works council leaders can avoid responsibility for unpleasant decisions. The trend towards stronger central works councils has been given strong support by the simultaneous centralisation of management in many large companies. Personnel management is becoming more centralised partly because of the introduction of more sophisticated methods of manpower planning. This has meant, however, that local works councils frequently find themselves without a counterpart with sufficient authority on the management side to negotiate with them. At Volkswagen, this pre-emption of local management authority was most obvious during the 1975 crisis when all important decisions concerning manpower policy were made by the central management, and local plant managers lost almost all their discretion in personnel matters.

The central works council at Volkswagen like the local works councils has its own resources that are made available by the company under a works agreement. The office of the central works council is in Wolfsburg. All members of the central works council are already released from normal work in their capacity as local works councillors. The central works council has, however, two full-time assistants (as well as two typists) who are paid for by the company but are appointed, and can be removed from their post, by the central works council. One of these, who serves as administrative assistant to the chairman of the central works council, is a former member of the Wolfsburg works council who in 1973 resigned his office to take his present position. Under the respective central works agreement, the assistants to the central works council get a salary which exceeds that of a Wolfsburg local works councillor. The second assistant is a professional journalist who edits a monthly newsletter informing the workforce of the central works council's activities. The costs of the newsletter are borne by the company which has no influence on its contents; in order to see its own views published, the company distributes a separate paper.

Even more so than at other companies, the IGM *Vertrauensleute* body at Volkswagen tends to be a functional extension of the works council rather than a political power centre in its own right. One reason for this is the size and the enormous resources of the works council which enable it to absorb all potentially independent *Vertrauensleute* leaders. Another is that mobilising political pressure through the *Vertrauensleute* is less important for IGM as a way of controlling the works council at Volkswagen than it is at other companies. An effective alternative to a strong *Vertrauensleute* body is the company agreement which makes for a closer than usual involvement of the union in company-specific matters. Moreover, the powerful position of the union on the supervisory board gives its headquarters a direct say in the running of the company and, in addition, creates a strong direct link between the works council and the national union leadership (see p. 54).

There are about 800 IGM *Vertrauensleute* at Wolfsburg. As with the works council, elections are held every three years. Each *Vertrauensmann* represents one workgroup. *Vertrauensleute* meet by departments and elect department councils. Members of department councils elect sectional councils, and sectional councillors elect a central *Vertrauensleute* council of which the IGM district secretary is an *ex officio* member. *Vertrauensleute* have the right to spend a certain number of paid hours per week on union business. Apart from the various councils, *Vertrauensleute* meetings are usually limited to the department level; it is only on rare occasions that all 800 Vertrauensleute meet together. The chairman of the central *Vertrauensleute* council is released from work just as if he were a works council member. His status, however, is clearly below that of a works councillor, and being elected works councillor would be considered an advancement.

Works meetings

Under Section 43,1 of the Works Constitution Act, the works council 'shall call a works meeting once in every calendar quarter' to report on its activities. Works meetings are composed of all employees of the establishment; they are chaired by the chairman of the works council. The law stipulates that works meetings 'shall be held during working hours' and that 'the time for attending the meetings . . . shall be remunerated as hours of work' (Section 44,1). The employer has a right to attend the meeting and is entitled to address it. In addition, he is obliged to give a yearly 'report to the works meeting on staff questions and social affairs in the establishment as well as on the financial position of the trends in the establishment, in so far as there is no risk of a disclosure of trade or business secrets' (Section 43,2).

The subjects works meetings can deal with are only broadly defined. Section 45 of the Act speaks of 'matters of direct concern to the establishment or the employees, including subjects in connection with collective bargaining policies, social policy and financial matters'. Although the Act states that in such discussions the principle of peaceful collaboration (Section 74,2) has to be observed, in effect it gives the works council and the union representatives the opportunity to put before a works meeting any matter which they feel to be important. By mentioning 'social policy', for example, the Act indirectly permits the introduction of political questions and thus provides an opportunity which is frequently made use of by the unions during general election campaigns.

Works meetings are not empowered to make decisions on any of the issues put before them. Formally, their powers are limited to making 'suggestions to the works council' and to taking 'a stand on its decisions'. In fact, however, the results of discussions at works meetings are taken very seriously by works councils, and if a works meeting expresses a strong opinion on a certain matter, it only rarely goes unheeded by the works council.

The IGM at Volkswagen: district and headquarters

The Wolfsburg district of IGM had nearly 18,000 members in 1965 and over 41,000 in 1975. The great majority of these were Volkswagen workers. At the same time, some of the IGM members at the Wolfsburg plant belong to IGM districts other than Wolfsburg. This is because part of the Volkswagen workforce commute over fairly long distances to their workplace. Although IGM members whose workplace is located in a district different from their residence have a choice, in principle, as to their place of organisation, the prevailing pattern seems to be that members belong to the district in which they live.

In addition to the Volkswagen plant, the IGM Wolfsburg district organises a small number of supplier firms and some car maintenance and repair shops. Although the internal life of the district is inevitably dominated by Volkswagen workers, special efforts are made to prevent Wolfsburg from becoming a one-plant district. Thus, care is taken that members who are not from Volkswagen are elected to the district assembly. Also, some residual local branch organisations are maintained to attend to workers from small companies with no, or only weak, workplace organisations.

Contacts between IGM and the Volkswagen works council especially if they are of political significance are maintained not through the district office – as would be the normal pattern – but directly by the national headquarters. This applies in particular to the provision of operational guidance in legal and economic matters, the exercise of co-determination rights, and negotiations with the company as well as to the nomination of candidates for works council elections. The reason for this departure from normal practice is that a union district office, however well-equipped, could not in any way match the enormous resources available to a works council as large as that at Volkswagen.

By the mid-1970s, contacts between the Volkswagen central works council and the union headquarters were maintained on the union side by an officer of the works councils department who served as the central liaison officer for four major companies. His primary concern, however, was Volkswagen and as a rule he spent about one week each month in Wolfsburg. Here, his functions ranged from giving legal and economic advice to the central works council, to participation in negotiations with the management. His main counterpart was the secretary of the central works council. When in 1978 the Co-determination Act of 1976 was implemented, IGM took the opportunity to strengthen the position of its Volkswagen liaison officer by nominating him, together with Loderer, as one of the three external workers' representatives on the supervisory board. For the union, this has the advantage that it not only helps to avoid duplication of effort but also serves to give the officer a legal status within the company and entitles him to confidential information from the management. It is primarily in this respect that the Co-determination Act of 1976 has brought significant advantages for the unions.

Politically and operationally the most important connection between the IGM and its workplace organisation at Volkswagen is that of the national union chairman on the one hand and the chairman of the Volkswagen central works council on the other. This link is institutionally supported by an arrangement which is reminiscent of an interlocking directorate. On the one hand the IGM chairman serves as the highest-ranking workers' representative on the Volkswagen supervisory board while the Volkswagen central works council chairman is traditionally elected by the IGM general conference as an unpaid member of the IGM national executive. This ensures that the interests of the Volkswagen workplace organisation are represented in a similarly prominent position within the IGM as are the interests of IGM at the national level *vis-à-vis* Volkswagen. The presence of Ehlers on the IGM executive, like the presence of Loderer on the Volkswagen supervisory board, expresses the importance assigned by IGM to Volkswagen as a company; it also takes account of the considerable power of the elected leader of a workforce as large as that at Volkswagen.

In preparing policy decisions relating to Volkswagen and in dealing with the Volkswagen workplace union, the chairman of the IGM can draw on two main sources of expert advice. The first is the economics department at IGM headquarters which is staffed with a number of university-trained economists. One of these, a former assistant professor of economics who went to IGM in the late 1960s, is responsible specifically for monitoring the car industry and the shipbuilding industry. During the Volkswagen crisis, he prepared several papers on the development and the future prospects of the car industry and was instrumental in putting the events at Volkswagen into an industry-wide perspective. Secondly, one of the three personal assistants to the IGM chairman – all of whom have doctoral degrees in economics – is in charge, among other things, of matters relating to the car industry in general and Volkswagen in particular. Having served for years as Loderer's principal adviser on Volkswagen, especially on the more operative aspects of policy, he was nominated and elected in the 1978 supervisory board elections, together with Loderer and the liaison officer from the works councils department, as the third external workers' representative at Volkswagen.

Footnotes

[1] The year in which the events described in Chapters 5, 6 and 7 began.

[2] A comparison made by the IGM car industry working team indicates that in March 1977 the average hourly wage rate at Volkswagen in Wolfsburg for 74 specified tasks was DM 12.68. This was higher than in all other 11 plants included in the study. The lead over the runner-up was seven *Pfennige*. Two *Pfennige* behind the runner-up came Volkswagen Hannover. However, the overall average of all 11 plants was DM 12.26 so that the average wage at Wolfsburg was only 3.4 per cent higher than the overall average. Volkswagen's lead was strongest among the skilled workers. Here again, the Wolfsburg plant paid most (DM 14.09) followed by the Hannover plant (DM 13.87). The difference between Wolfsburg and the third-ranking plant (DM 13.83) was 26 *Pfennige*.

5 The 1975 Volkswagen Redundancy Scheme

The early 1970s were a period of economic crisis for Volkswagen. In 1974, losses ran as high as DM 555 million (£139 million at 1980 exchange rates). To restore profitability, the company in the following year decided to reduce the workforce of its German plants by 18,500, that is, by 17 per cent. The following account describes the events leading up to this decision and analyses the reactions of the union, IGM, and the Volkswagen works council to the measures taken by management.

The Volkswagen crisis of 1974 and 1975 was the result of year-long mismanagement on the one hand, combined with the general crisis in the car industry after the 1973 oil embargo, on the other. There were mainly three management-related causes of the company's decline which gradually began to take effect from about 1970.

(i) During the 1960s, Volkswagen had become too dependent on exports particularly to the United States. To an extent, the company shared this problem with the West German economy as a whole. The main reason for the strong export-orientation of both Volkswagen and the West German national economy, was the undervaluation of the German Mark. This led to large trade surpluses throughout the 1950s and 1960s and to a disproportionate growth in the manufacturing sector, resulting in what was frequently referred to as an 'over-industrialisation' of the West German economy.

As for Volkswagen, one of the crucial mistakes the management made in the 1960s was that they did nothing to prevent the share of production sold on the North American market from becoming even higher. As a result, in 1970 no less than 35 per cent of all German-produced Volkswagen cars went to the United States. One of the six German Volkswagen plants, Emden, worked exclusively for export to the US. It is obvious that this made the company extremely vulnerable to changes in the exchange rate and to any other political or economic development reducing its competitive advantages on the US market.

In the early 1970s, several such developments occurred more or less at the same time. First of all, in late 1969 the Mark was revalued for the first time since 1945. Several more revaluations followed. In 1973, the fixed exchange rate system finally broke down and was replaced by a system of floating exchange rates. Secondly, during the recovery from the general economic crisis of 1967 and 1968, and in the wake of the change of government in 1969, wages in Germany had risen steeply. Although Volkswagen wages in the late 1960s were already about 23 per cent higher than in the rest of the engineering industry they too increased significantly. Both the revaluation of the Mark and the growing labour costs made Volkswagen less competitive in the United States. As Volkswagen cars became more expensive for American buyers, the number of cars sold in the United States began to decline steadily. Whereas in 1970 about 570,000 Volkswagens were sold in the US, in 1974 sales were down to 334,000 or 27 per cent of the total production. Two years later, in 1976, US sales had fallen to no more than 205,000 cars, that is, about 16 per cent of the total output (Table 5.1).

Table 5.1   Volkswagen AG(a): Number of Cars Sold in the United States

	Cars sold (000s)	As per cent of all cars sold
1970	570	35
1971	523	31
1972	486	33
1973	476	33
1974	334	27
1975	279	26
1976	205	16

(a) Excluding Audi NSU and foreign subsidiaries

(ii) Because of the tremendous success of the Beetle, the Volkswagen management in the 1960s failed to provide for product diversification or to prepare for the introduction of new models. Up to the death in 1968 of the first managing director after the war, Heinrich Nordhoff, the company was content to produce one model, the Beetle. This policy of maintaining what was called by critics the 'Beetle monoculture' began to create serious problems at a time when the Beetle still sold well. The reason was that although the basic design of the Beetle was not changed, it had to be amended almost every year to meet competition and to satisfy increased safety and environmental standards. In the latter respect, the company, because of its large exports to the United States, was severely affected by the US legislation of the early 1970s. As a result, the Beetle, because of a long series of incremental modifications and improvements, became increasingly complex and costly to produce. Although, by the early 1970s, the Beetle had become a surprisingly sophisticated car, productivity at Volkswagen, according to an IGM report, declined between 1968 and 1973 by no less than 17 per cent.[1]

(iii) In 1968, Volkswagen took over NSU, a small, loss-making car producer in Southern Germany, which was later merged with another Volkswagen subsidiary, Audi. There were three main reasons for the take-over. One was the expectation that the market would continue to expand and that Volkswagen would need additional capacity. Moreover, NSU was a competitor on the German small cars market. Finally, and perhaps most importantly, NSU was one of the more innovative car producers in Germany which had invented, among other things, the Wankel engine. Obviously, one idea behind the NSU take-over was that the technical know-how of NSU could be used to facilitate the impending model change at Volkswagen.

The reason why the acquisition of NSU turned out to be less profitable than expected was primarily the lack of a clear strategy at Volkswagen with regard to the introduction of a successor model to the Beetle. Since Volkswagen continued to produce the Beetle, and since Beetle sales began to stagnate so that no new capacity was necessary, NSU had to continue to produce its old models. As a result, it continued to make losses.

The model problem

The foremost problem the new management after 1968 had to deal with was that of the emerging model crisis. Although the Beetle had become increasingly costly to build, at the time of the take-over of the new general manager, Kurt Lotz, no successor model was in sight. Hard-pressed for a speedy decision Lotz, instead of replacing the Beetle completely by a whole new set of models, decided to introduce several different models alongside the Beetle.[2] None of these, except those built by the Audi subsidiary, were a success. Moreover, all of them were designed differently and were technically incompatible. This made it impossible to use identical components to achieve economies of scale.

Despite declining profits, the 'model pluralism' at Volkswagen continued well into the early 1970s. When in 1971 it became obvious that Lotz was unable to simplify the model structure and to manage the transition to a successor model to the Beetle, he was replaced by the managing director of Audi, Herman Leiding. During Leiding's time as managing director of Volkswagen, which lasted until 1974, a comprehensive new model system was introduced. The new models, which were based on the cars that later came to be known as the Passat and the Golf, had been developed at Audi under Leiding's leadership. Leiding's first and central decision as Volkswagen general manager was that these models were to be produced and marketed not under the Audi but under the Volkswagen label. Apart from their attractiveness to the customers – which had already been demonstrated by their predecessor models at Audi – they were very economical to produce. Many components were interchangeable among the different models, and the number of components was much lower than with the Beetle. While the first factor promised economies of scale, the second meant an increase in productivity.

The introduction of the new models, however, took time. Meanwhile, the economic situation of the company deteriorated significantly. In addition to losing out on its traditional export markets, Volkswagen experienced a decline of its market share in Germany. Production in 1972 was 14 per cent below the 1971 level, profits fell to an all-time low of DM86 million (less than one per cent of total sales; Table 5.2), and employment in the German plants declined by 14,000 workers or 11 per cent of the total workforce. Since the economy as a whole was still expanding in 1972, the reduction of employment could be achieved without much difficulty by natural wastage and severance payments.

Table 5.2   Volkswagen AG(a): Economic Performance

	1972	1973	1974	1975	1976
Sales (*DM million*)	10,399	11,563	11,219	11,370	16,914
Cars sold (*000s*)	1,472	1,448	1,238	1,048	1,315
Profits after tax (*DM million*)	86	109	−555	−145	789
Dividend (*DM million*)	81	81	—	—	90
Investment (*DM million*)	785	755	1,207	374	332
Staff expenses (*DM million*)	3,136	3,699	3,940	3,593	4,291

(a) Excluding Audi NSU and foreign subsidiaries

The impact of the 1973 crisis

The first of the new Volkswagens appeared on the market in early 1973. However, sales remained almost the same as in the year before. With hindsight, this is in line with the observation that the car boom had reached its climax well before the Arab oil embargo, and that the oil crisis was just one more factor adding to a general crisis in the car industry which would have developed in any case. Other major German car producers experienced a decline or stagnation of sales in early 1973. Despite these indications, however, Leiding believed that with the introduction of the new models another Volkswagen boom was imminent. To meet the expected increase in demand, the company took on 9,000 new workers, expanding its domestic workforce to about 126,000 (Table 5.3). However, demand did not increase but rather, as a result of the crisis and under the impact of the oil embargo, declined (Table 5.2). Although sales revenues went up considerably because the prices of

Table 5.3   Employment at Volkswagen AG(a)

End year, thousands

	1973	1974	1975	1976
Total	125.8	111.5	93.0	97.4
Wolfsburg	56.5	51.2	46.1	48.9
Hannover	26.5	21.6	16.9	17.3
Braunschweig	7.0	6.0	4.9	5.2
Kassel	18.8	16.4	13.7	13.9
Emden	7.6	7.3	6.1	6.5
Salzgitter	9.4	9.1	5.3	5.6
Blue-collar	110.9	96.6	79.1	83.6
White-collar	14.9	14.9	13.8	13.8
Female	15.3	13.4	10.3	11.0
Foreign nationals	20.0	13.4	6.9	7.3
Apprentices	1.8	1.9	1.9	2.2
Average age (years)	37.5	38.7	39.7	39.4
Average length of service (years)	9.5	10.9	12.4	12.5
Sickness rate (days)	7.4	6.0	5.3	6.4

(a) Excluding Audi NSU and foreign subsidiaries

cars had increased, profits remained almost constant, owing to the increased wage bill. This situation was all the more serious since Volkswagen, in connection with the ongoing model change, continued to have high investment needs. Although the company had invested DM 785 million in 1972 and DM 755 million in 1973, the transition to the new models was far from complete. Given the continuing low profitability of the company and the uncertain prospects of the industry, financing the new investment was bound to become increasingly difficult.

Although 1973 had in no way improved the condition of the company, the management clung to its optimistic expectations. As demand on the German market remained low, hopes for an imminent boom were centred on the United States. As a result of the higher price of gasoline, the Volkswagen management expected an increased demand by American buyers for compact economical cars and this would allow Volkswagen to regain its previous market share. To be prepared for this, another 2,500 workers were hired in the first three months of 1974 although several German Volkswagen plants at this time were already doing short-time work.

Reduction of employment
In April 1974, it became clear that the expected boom was not likely to

materialise either in Germany or the United States. In fact, 1974 was to become the worst year ever for the company. The number of cars sold went down by 15 per cent to 1,238 million (Table 5.2). Whereas, in the year before, higher prices had made for an increase of revenue in spite of declining sales, in 1974 revenue fell by about 3 per cent. At the same time, investment into the new models had to be increased by about 60 per cent to DM 1,207 million. As a result, the company lost DM 555 million.

When it had become obvious that the situation was deteriorating, one of the first measures the management took was to reduce the workforce. First, a general recruitment ban was imposed, and workers were transferred within plants to fill gaps caused by natural wastage. Also, fixed term contracts with foreign workers were not renewed. Two months later (in June/July), severance payments were offered ranging from DM 5,000–10,000 and workers over 62 years of age were offered early retirement, with the company making up the difference in their expected pensions. The campaign was stopped in late July, but had to be started again in October. This time, the early retirement age was lowered to 59. By the end of the year, the company's domestic workforce was reduced by 14,300 (about 12 per cent) 7,400 of whom had taken severance payments.[3]

Although employment at Volkswagen by the end of 1974 had fallen below the 1972 level, this was not yet considered sufficient. Compared to the year before, the expectations of the management had become more pessimistic. This view was shared by the banks which were supposed to finance the new investment and who believed that further employment cuts were necessary to get the company through the transition period and restore its profitability. It was the managing director, in particular, who made a point of emphasising publicly as well as in his contacts with the union and the works council the need for a further reduction of manpower, if necessary through forced redundancies. In addition and at the same time, Leiding once more began to press his idea that the only way of regaining the company's former position in the North American market was to set up a manufacturing plant in the United States.

One interesting aspect of the manpower policy of the Leiding era concerns the employment of foreign labour. When Volkswagen in 1973 and early 1974 hired a total of 11,500 new workers, few German workers were available. Thus the new workers were mainly foreign nationals. Similarly, when the company reduced its labour force in the following year, foreign workers were vastly over-represented among those whose employment was terminated. In fact, the number of foreign nationals working at Volkswagen declined in 1974 by one-third and almost fell back to the 1972 level (Table 5.3).

Although it might be suspected that the high turnover among foreign workers in 1973 and 1974 was the result of a deliberate strategy of discrimination, upon closer inspection the matter turns out to be rather more complex. While Volkswagen at the time did in fact have fixed-term contracts with foreign workers, the clear majority were on normal work contracts. Today, as a result of action taken by the works council, fixed-term contracts have completely disappeared so that all workers enjoy the same legal employment protection.

One explanation why so many foreign workers left Volkswagen in 1974 is the composition of the company's foreign labour force. To reduce language problems and to minimise political and cultural conflicts between different national groups, Volkswagen from early on employed workers from only one foreign country, Italy. It was only in the late 1960s and early 1970s when Italian labour became scarce that a small number of Tunisians were taken on in addition. Since Italy is a member of the European Community, Italian workers have the same legal rights in Germany as German workers. In particular, they cannot be sent back to their country when their contract of employment has ended, and they can re-enter Germany whenever they wish without having to apply for readmission. In the case of Volkswagen, this meant that almost the entire foreign labour force could afford to take the severance payment and either return home or take up new employment with another company. Since in 1974 the demand for labour in the German economy was still high, the latter was relatively easy – especially because foreign workers are for obvious reasons much more willing than German workers to move to another place of residence within Germany. Thus, given the structure of the foreign workforce at Volkswagen, it is not surprising that a large number of foreign workers were prepared to take severance payments and give up their jobs voluntarily.

The effect of the reduction of employment on the structure of the workforce can be seen in Table 5.3. Apart from the disproportionate reduction of the foreign workforce, the most conspicuous aspect of the change between 1973 and 1974 was that the decline affected only the blue-collar group while the number of white-collar workers remained constant. Generally, the average age of the labour force increased, as did the average length of service – indicating that younger workers with less seniority decided to leave their jobs at a higher rate than older workers with a longer period of service.

The end of the Leiding era
By the end of 1974, both the shareholders and the workers' representatives on the Volkswagen supervisory board had lost confidence in the managing director and had started searching for a successor. Among the supervisory board members as well as among the general public,

Leiding at this time was seen as a brilliant engineer – he was an engineer by training – who unfortunately seemed to be an inept businessman and manager. Leiding himself had done much to contribute to this image. On the one hand, he had undoubtedly played the key role in the development of the new and much acclaimed model series. On the other hand, he had several times misjudged the market, had long underestimated the seriousness of the company's crisis, and had taken to a 'hire and fire' employment policy which had cost him not only considerable sums of money but also the goodwill of the works council and the IGM.

Generally, Leiding's policy in relation to the works council and the union appears to have been to limit their role to the minimum of consultation and co-determination prescribed by the law. For a while, this seems to have caused no major problems. While the works council undoubtedly disliked the 'hiring and firing' in 1973 and early 1974, it was not overly concerned about it. Volkswagen had not had major redundancy problems in the past, and the works council not only had no experience in such situations but also shared, at least initially, the generally optimistic expectations of the management. Moreover, as long as the general labour market was still relatively tight, and as long as there was a sizeable group of foreign workers who were prepared to take severance payments, even the employment cutback in 1974 did not seem to be a reason for alarm.

This started to change when it turned out during 1974 that the crisis was there to stay and that there was even the possibility of forced redundancies coinciding with rising general unemployment. For the Volkswagen works council, like many other works councils of major German enterprises, manpower policy, on the eve of the crisis of the mid-1970s, began to assume a new and hitherto unknown significance. Against this background, the fact that Leiding preferred to conduct the company's manpower policy with as little works council involvement as possible became less and less acceptable.

By the end of 1974, Leiding's attitude towards the works council, and the tensions resulting from it, were seen as a serious problem by most of the shareholders' representatives on the supervisory board. Given the likely need for further employment cuts which could probably be achieved only by forced dismissals, a managing director who during the preceding one and a half years had never even met the works council, increasingly appeared as a liability. As the crisis of the company was approaching its peak, one of the central concerns of the shareholders came to be whether the managing director would be able to get the co-operation of the union and the works council for the necessary reorganisation measures. With Leiding, this appeared extremely unlikely. It was for this reason more than for any other that a consensus emerged among the shareholders in the second half of 1974 to look for a successor.

The new Managing Director

The key role in the replacement of Leiding was played by the Federal government. As one of the major shareholders, the government was directly interested in the company's economic viability. More importantly, a breakdown of Volkswagen would have caused a major crisis on the labour market which would have posed considerable problems for the government. The matter also had a highly significant symbolic dimension. Volkswagen had for years been the symbol of the success of the German economy; had it faltered, this would have had unpredictable consequences for the general political and psychological climate. Last but not least, since the Federal government at this time was under Social-Democratic control it had a vital interest in preventing the problems of Volkswagen leading to open conflict between union and management. From early on, partly to fend off allegations by the opposition of 'socialist mismanagement' and partly because of its own political convictions, the government had been against public subsidisation of Volkswagen and in favour of what was called a 'private enterprise solution'. For the latter to be possible without disruptions, however, co-operative relations between the management and the workers' representatives were of vital importance.

It is interesting to note how closely the events at Volkswagen were followed by the Federal government. For example, when Leiding in 1973 decided to take on additional labour, the then Minister of Finance, Helmut Schmidt, personally urged him 'not to hire new workers, particularly workers from abroad'. This advice, according to Schmidt in 1975 in a speech as Chancellor to the Bundestag, 'was not heeded'. In the spring of 1974, Schmidt again, in his own words, 'went to great lengths to persuade the Volkswagen management that it was unreasonable to expect that the increase in the price of gasoline would lead to increased Volkswagen sales in the United States. . . My advice was not taken. . .' After this meeting, Schmidt 'came to the conclusion that a change of management was inevitable.'

However, although the Federal government in many respects played a leading role among the Volkswagen shareholders, it was by itself not strong enough to bring about an immediate change. Rather than asking straight out for Leiding's resignation, the Finance Minister first pressed for the resignation of the chairman of the supervisory board who had brought Leiding in. This was because the transition to a new managing director would have been difficult to effect from outside the company and without the active support of the appropriate company body. Nevertheless, it was only in November of 1974 that the pressure exerted by the government finally took effect and the chairman of the supervisory board resigned. According to Schmidt, 'we then used the new situation on the supervisory board to change the composition of the management board. . . . I admit there was a very strong influence exerted by the minority shareholder, the Federal government, to bring about this change. Otherwise, we would never have arrived at a reorganisation strategy for this company.'

The new chairman of the supervisory board, who was appointed on the proposal of the Federal government, was the managing director of Salzgitter AG, Herr Birnbaum. Salzgitter is a large steel and engineering conglomerate, owned by the Federal government. (Since supervisory board positions are not full-time, Birnbaum retained his position at Salzgitter.) In his post at Salzgitter, Birnbaum had gained as much experience as anybody else in running a government-controlled enterprise. While this made him in a sense a representative of the public sector or even of the Federal government, it is characteristic of the kind of crisis solution that was envisaged that the government did not propose a civil servant as supervisory board chairman but rather a professional manager.

The search for a new managing director was rapid and was conducted with the strong involvement of Helmut Schmidt who by this time had become Chancellor. Even more than in his former office, it was now of crucial political importance for Schmidt that the Volkswagen crisis should be solved as soon as possible. In late December 1974, the Volkswagen supervisory board on the proposal of its chairman appointed Toni Schmücker, then managing director of Rheinstahl, as Leiding's successor. Schmücker took up his new post on 20 January 1975.

There were several reasons why Schmücker appeared almost ideally qualified for the Volkswagen position. One was that up to 1968 he had been a successful sales director with Ford Germany and thus knew the car industry. Secondly, when in 1968 Schmücker took over at Rheinstahl – one of the biggest German steel concerns – the company was almost bankrupt. As managing director, Schmücker developed and implemented a comprehensive reorganisation programme which led to the company's complete recovery. The Rheinstahl crisis had been broadly covered by the media, and Schmücker had become known to the public as 'the reorganiser'. Thirdly, since Rheinstahl, like all companies in the coal and steel industry, is subject to supervisory board co-determination, during his time there Schmücker had learned to come to terms with a union with considerable institutional power. At Volkswagen, where the position of the union resembled more the coal and steel type of co-determination than the pattern in the rest of German industry, this seemed to be exactly what was needed, especially in a situation in which difficult and painful decisions were inevitable.

That Schmücker had in fact handled the co-determination system at Rheinstahl exceedingly well is shown by the reaction of the IGM officials to his proposed appointment. When asked for their opinion of Schmücker, the IGM leadership sought the advice of the Rheinstahl works council and were told that Schmücker had made a point of fully informing the works council on his plans and decisions; that he had given careful consideration to the works council's and the union's opinion; and that he had been a tough but reliable counterpart in negotiations. On the basis of this information, the works representatives on the supervisory board voted in favour of Schmücker's appointment.

The situation at Schmücker's take-over

When Schmücker took up his new post in late January 1975, he was able to start, in at least three respects, from a relatively favourable position. For one thing, he had the strong backing of the Federal government and, in particular, the Chancellor. Furthermore, most of the investment for the new models had been made and it was possible to reduce overall investment by about 70 per cent to a normal DM 374 million as the transition to the new models was almost complete. Whereas in January 1974, 54 per cent of all cars built in Wolfsburg had been Beetles, in June of that year the Beetle at this plant was phased out. In Emden, where at the beginning of 1974 all car production has consisted of Beetles, by the end of that year, their share in the output had declined to 41 per cent. Finally, in February 1975 works council elections were held, and the re-elected works councillors had a full three-years' term of office before them. If the union and the works council were at all prepared to accept 'economic realities', then this was the time when they were most likely to do so.

The most pressing, and indeed formidable, problem Schmücker had to tackle was that of adapting the company's productive capacity to the market. In early 1975, there was widespread agreement that the workforce at Volkswagen was too large for current production requirements and that the wage bill was excessive. The latter, of course, was not only the result of overmanning and low productivity; it was also due to the strong bargaining position of the union. This is demonstrated, among other things, by the fact that in spite of a considerable reduction of the workforce, total staff expenses at Volkswagen in 1974 increased by 6.5 per cent (Table 5.2).[4]

Foremost among those who pressed for a reduction of the wage bill were the banks. Some of the leading members of the Volkswagen supervisory board were managing directors of large banks, and there is no doubt that they used their position to force their priorities on the new management. According to reports in the press, it was in particular the representative of the Deutsche Bank, Herr Christians, who pointed to the probable cash-flow problems and demanded 'vigorously' a fast and lasting solution. Although Schmücker, on taking up office, had kept up the existing recruitment ban, called short-time work in all German plants, and continued the severance payments programme, these measures were not considered strong enough either by himself or by the banks. What their representatives expected was not a continuation of the old manpower policy but a comprehensive, detailed plan for a speedy and lasting employment reduction. It was obvious that the first task for the new managing director was to devise a strategy by which this expectation could be met.

During the Leiding era, manpower policy at Volkswagen had been conducted without much participation by either the works council or the supervisory board. This was possible because the instruments used to reduce employment – such as recruitment bans, natural wastage, severance payments and early retirement – are neither subject to co-determination by the works council nor require the assent of the supervisory board. There are reasons to believe that this was why these instruments were preferred to others by the Leiding management board. With Schmücker's take-over, this policy changed. Whereas Leiding seems to have chosen his manpower policy instruments in order to minimise the role of the works council and the supervisory board, Schmücker from the beginning consulted the two bodies on any matter of importance regardless of whether or not he was legally obliged to do so. This applied in particular to the supervisory board which included the chairman of the central works council. This approach responded to traditional union demands for an extension of the jurisdiction of supervisory boards in relation to the management. As a result, the supervisory board at Volkswagen in the following years became the central policy-making body of the company acting on matters which in other companies the management would have been careful to reserve for itself.

The K1 scheme

The first matter on which the management was to ask the supervisory board's approval was employment reduction. Upon taking office, Schmücker had charged the personnel department with developing several alternative plans to reduce the workforce. One of these, labelled 'K1', provided for a reduction of the workforce by 30,000 reducing the total workforce to 81,000. The scheme also included the complete shutdown of the NSU plants. This alone would have made 11,500 workers redundant. There are indications that Schmücker initially favoured K1 over its alternatives. However, he took care not to identify himself with it publicly. Instead, the scheme was informally leaked to the press, and it was immediately rejected and criticised as unfair and irresponsible by the works council and the IGM.

In the weeks after the publication of K1, public attention focused almost exclusively on the intended shutdown of NSU. It was particularly the IGM *Bezirk* of Baden-Württemberg – where all NSU plants are located – which became the centre of the opposition to K1. No strikes were called, however, mainly because the union felt that closing down a plant through a strike was not a very logical way of protecting it from being closed by the management.[5] Instead, several big demonstrations were organised and local politicians were urged to come to the workers' support. The most remarkable success of the IGM in this respect was that it got the Prime Minister of the Land of Baden-Württemberg, Hans Karl Filbinger – a right-wing Christian Democrat – to join the campaign to save NSU; Filbinger accused the central Volkswagen management of 'irresponsible job destruction'.

Backed by the developments in Baden-Württemberg, and pressed by his own regional officials, the chairman of IGM, Eugen Loderer, let Schmücker know that any reorganisation plan which included closing down NSU was unacceptable to the union. The reasons why this stand was taken so uncompromisingly reflect the political imperatives of industrial unionism. From a narrow Volkswagen perspective the decision to defend NSU at any price would not have been self-evident, and in making this decision, IGM in fact incurred considerable risks of internal conflict. Had it been up to the Volkswagen central works council only, the closure of NSU would have appeared as no more than a minor evil; jobs abolished at NSU were first and foremost jobs saved at Volkswagen plants. Since NSU at this time had about 12,000 workers, its closure would have significantly relieved the pressure at Volkswagen and might have helped as many as 8,000 Volkswagen workers to keep their jobs. NSU was a comparatively recent acquisition of the Volkswagen company – an acquisition which was felt by some to have been a mistake by an inept management. It was not a profitable concern and it was probable that it would remain unprofitable for some time. There were good reasons, therefore, why workers' representatives at Volkswagen should not have been particularly eager to sacrifice jobs at their own plants to keep NSU 'artificially' alive.

These reasons did not apply, however, from the perspective of the IGM as an industrial union. The constituency of the IGM leadership includes not just the workforce at Volkswagen but the workforce in the entire engineering industry. The cohesion of an industrial union depends on its ability to develop and maintain an internal compromise between the different sectional interests of its members. This requires that all groups are offered about the same amount of protection; that no group enjoys privileges which are not also, at least in principle, made available to other groups; and that while all groups may be asked to make sacrifices on behalf of others, no group must be asked to sacrifice itself. That these principles are in fact followed is ensured, among other things, by the primacy of the territorial over the workplace organisation and by the structure of the territorial organisation itself. It is remarkable that throughout the Volkswagen crisis, there never was an open disagreement – and probably not even a hidden one – between the Volkswagen works council and the IGM leadership on whether or not NSU should be defended. This testifies to the considerable political skills of the IGM leadership in dealing with internal conflicts of interest. By establishing from early on that a shutdown of NSU would run into vigorous opposition from the union, Loderer may have disappointed some of his Volkswagen members; on the other hand, he stabilised his support in Baden-Württemberg, and he demonstrated to the IGM membership at large that although their union may sometimes have to neglect some of their immediate, short-term interests, when it came to essentials it would do its utmost to afford them the solidarity of the entire organisation.

On the other hand, Loderer in his response to K1 made clear that he recognised the need for Volkswagen to recover its profitability. He also indicated that he was aware that this would involve further reductions in the workforce. From his contacts with the Federal government, and in particular with the Chancellor, Loderer knew for certain that there would be no subsidisation of Volkswagen from public funds, however much the situation might deteriorate. Moreover at the time of the Volkswagen crisis a Bill was before the Bundestag which provided for the extension of the coal and steel type of co-determination. Since co-determination at Volkswagen was more akin to that in coal and steel than to that in private industry generally, opponents of the Bill had already begun to cite the company as an example of the decline the German economy would suffer as a consequence of extension of co-determination. In this situation, the IGM felt it politically expedient to demonstrate that a strong position of the union on the supervisory board does not delay necessary managerial action – even if painful for the workforce – and, in particular, does not impede profitability. For IGM to be able to show this, however, the management had to offer a reorganisation scheme in which the burden was as equally distributed among the different sectors of the workforce as possible. It was this message which the union tried to get across to the management when it registered its unconditional opposition to the K1 scheme.[6]

It is important to note that for the IGM, the relationship between co-determination and 'responsible' behaviour was, and is, far more than a matter of political tactics. IGM, and in particular its leaders, are well aware that institutionalised influence on economic decisions implies that, in the words of an IGM official interviewed for this study, 'one cannot content oneself with just saying "No" '. Like the other unions affiliated to the DGB, IGM not only supports the principle of co-determination but also accepts that it brings with it responsibility. 'Economic realities', to quote the IGM official once more, 'exist regardless of co-determination'. Having gained a right to continuous information on and involvement in management decisions, the union cannot but consider the consequences of its proposals and deal with a company's problems in a 'constructive' and 'realistic' way. Most important in this respect is the practical obligation resulting from co-determination to present the membership with the unpleasant as well as the pleasant aspects of a given situation, and to defend against 'irresponsible' criticism the decisions made under union participation and influence. In this sense, Eugen Loderer in a newspaper interview shortly after the supervisory board decision emphasised that, 'his union will continue to do what it can to work against a radicalisation, resulting from despair, among the Volkswagen workforce'.[7]

The S1 scheme

When the strongly negative response of the union to K1 had become apparent, the management publicly disowned the plan and instead proposed, as its first official statement of intent, what came to be known during the course of events as the 'S1 Scheme'. Since the IGM had maintained that K1 had been the managements' preferred policy, S1 could be presented to the membership as a result of union resistance and, in this sense, as a first important success.

The most important feature of S1 was that NSU was to remain in operation. Otherwise, the scheme envisaged a reduction of the total workforce by 25,000 – 18.5 per cent – within two years. Most strongly affected were the assembly plant at Brussels which stood to lose 45 per cent of its workers, and Neckarsulm (NSU) where the cuts were to be as high as 41 per cent (Table 5.4). Another considerable reduction was proposed for the Salzgitter plant whose workforce was to be cut by more than one-third (36 per cent). Relatively small cuts were planned for the Audi plant at Ingolstadt (10.6 per cent) and the main Volkswagen plant at Wolfsburg (12 per cent). The scheme made it incumbent on the managements of the individual plants to implement the reductions in accordance with local conditions. To achieve their quotas, managements were to rely primarily on natural wastage, severance payments and early retirement. Only in cases where these instruments proved insufficient were forced dismissals to be used. The maximum number of forced dismissals throughout the company was to be 10,000.

While the management could have implemented its scheme on its

Table 5.4   Employment after the SI Scheme, April 1975

	Employment at April 1975	Target of SI scheme	Planned reduction	
			Number	Per cent
Volkswagen(a)	105,480	88,000	17,480	16.6
Wolfsburg	48,700	42,800	5,900	12.1
Hannover	20,700	16,800	3,900	18.8
Braunschweig	5,780	4,900	880	15.2
Kassel	15,100	12,800	2,300	15.2
Emden	6,900	5,400	1,500	21.7
Salzgitter	8,300	5,300	3,000	36.1
Brussels	3,000	1,650	1,350	45.0
Audi NSU	27,500	21,100	6,400	23.3
Ingolstadt	16,000	14,300	1,700	10.6
Neckarsulm	11,500	6,800	4,700	40.9
Total(a)	132,980	109,100	23,880	18.0

(a) Excluding Brussels

own, Schmücker had made it clear from the beginning that he would not act without the assent of the supervisory board. The meeting at which SI was to be discussed was scheduled for 15 April. In the preceding six weeks, the IGM had time to analyse the proposal. After internal discussions, the union decided to oppose SI and develop an alternative. Whereas the management had envisaged a reduction of the workforce by 25,000, the union maintained that a cutback by 20,000 was sufficient. Of these, 4,700 at most were to be involuntarily dismissed, and the forced redundancies were to be spread evenly over the second half of 1975 and the whole of 1976. The latter was to apply also to severance payments and early retirement. Moreover, in case the economic conditions improved, under the union plan, former Volkswagen workers who had lost or given up their jobs were to have priority if and when new workers were taken on.

The alternative scheme proposed by the union was based on more optimistic assumptions about the future of the car market than those of the management. Officially, the union took the position that a new car boom was in the offing, and that the problem facing Volkswagen was not one of adjusting to a generally lower level of sales and production, but merely one of buying time until the market recovered. It is interesting to note that in advance of the supervisory board meeting, the IGM

and the management made repeated attempts to reconcile their conflicting expectations on the development of the market. On several
occasions, the car experts from the union's Economics Department and
from the chairman's office at IGM headquarters went to Wolfsburg to
meet the staff of the Volkswagen sales department. However, no agreement was reached. While the union upheld its optimistic view, the
representatives of the management stuck to their pessimistic assumptions, and neither side was able to produce convincing evidence to make
the other side change its mind.

The preparation of the supervisory board decision

When the discussion between the experts had failed to produce consensus, it was clear that the management would present S1 to the supervisory board and ask for a majority decision. For the union, this meant
that if it wanted to force through its alternative proposal, it had to press
the two governments represented on the board – the Federal government and the Land of Niedersachsen government – to have their
representatives vote against the management. This course of action was
favoured by the Volkswagen central works council. Since Niedersachsen was likely to follow the lead of the Federal government, the
chairman of the central works council and a number of works council
representatives went to Bonn to see the Finance Minister (who, unlike
the Economics Minister, was a Social Democrat). At their request,
Loderer went along – although he knew that the Federal government
was unwilling to subsidise Volkswagen and that the Chancellor was
prepared to let the management have its way. In the event, as Loderer
had expected, the Finance Minister pointed out to the Volkswagen
delegation that the government preferred S1 to the union alternative,
and that in any case it could not politically afford to refuse the new
managing director the confidence of the shareholders so shortly after
his taking office.

It is no exaggeration to say that the Volkswagen crisis was the one
dominating theme at IGM headquarters during the first months of
1975, both in a technical and in a political sense. Technically, two
economic experts, one from the Economics Department and the other
from the chairman's office, devoted almost all of their time to Volkswagen. Particularly time-consuming was the preparation for the supervisory board meetings. For one such meeting, the union experts had to
compile a list of about 100 specific questions with which to confront the
management; by thus forcing the management to produce evidence in
support of its plan, the union hoped to discover the weak spots in the
management's case.

In political terms, the events at Volkswagen once again opened up
IGM's perennial problem of organisational unity. From the viewpoint

of the leadership, the Volkswagen crisis harboured an explosive conflict potential between the organised Volkswagen workers on the one hand and the rest of the membership on the other. If the union had taken a 'narrow', 'sectional', 'syndicalist' Volkswagen position – demanding the preservation of jobs at Volkswagen at any price, even at the price of abandoning NSU or subsidisation from the taxpayer – it would have set a dangerous precedent. Other members in other companies, when in the same economic situation, would have asked for the same kind of protection. Especially in the case of public subsidies, this would have required a complete reversal of the union's traditional attitude on economic and technological change, and in the long run it would have undermined the economic basis of its wage policy. Moreover, since the IGM as a (multi) industrial union has to be responsive to the interests of a highly heterogeneous membership, it would have had to face the question of why its other members – for example, the workers of other car companies – should, in their capacity as taxpayers, pay to support an unprofitable car manufacturer. For these and similar reasons, it was a matter of political necessity for the IGM not to identify itself too closely with the immediate interests of the Volkswagen workers, and to put the Volkswagen problems into a broader industrial, or even national, context.

On the other hand, Volkswagen is one of the most important companies organised by IGM and the Volkswagen workers are perhaps the most powerful single group among the membership. Just as the union could not afford to alienate its other members by identifying itself with special Volkswagen interests, it could not afford either to give the Volkswagen workers the impression that they were only half-heartedly supported by their union. There was at times what an IGM official referred to as a 'poisoned atmosphere' at Volkswagen – a climate of rumours, suspicion and even panic. To counteract thus, Loderer and Ehlers in advance of the March supervisory board meeting attended works assemblies in all Volkswagen plants to explain and, if necessary, defend their joint policy. This seems to have been successful. When the supervisory board met to consider the management's S1 scheme, union and works council had succeeded in building up a common position which was unchallenged by any major group among the workforce.

The decision

When, after long discussion, the supervisory board voted on S1, the management's proposal was carried by 14 votes to 7. The 7 dissenters were the workers' representatives including the chairman of the IGM, Eugen Loderer. Among the majority were the representatives of the two governments and the managing director of the Bank für Gemeinwirtschaft, Hesselbach. According to press reports, it was the bankers' arguments which made the strongest impression on the government representatives. For the two governments, the foremost concern obviously was not to be responsible for Volkswagen falling into a cash crisis. When it was indicated by the bank representatives that without a drastic reorganisation plan, Volkswagen might come to be considered a credit risk,[8] the union alternative had lost whatever slim chances of success it may still have had, and the final vote was a mere formality.

After the decision, there was some public speculation as to how serious the opposition of the workers' representatives to the S1 scheme actually had been. One hypothesis was that the dissenting votes had been just window-dressing, and that behind closed doors the union had long since signalled to the management that it by and large accepted S1. Others went so far as to suggest that S1 had in fact been tacitly negotiated between the two sides and represented an informal compromise which the IGM, while not wanting to confess to it publicly, had promised to let pass. The strongest evidence in favour of such speculations was that Hesselbach had voted with the shareholders – which showed that at least one prominent union figure appreciated the position taken by the banks. Moreover, the union had let it be known from early on that now that the closure of NSU was no longer on the agenda, it would accept the outcome of the supervisory board decision either way, and that it would not call upon its membership to fight the decision if it went in favour of the management.

Another point made in support of the window-dressing theory is less convincing. If the S1 scheme is compared to the union alternative, it could be argued that the difference in the number of redundancies was so small that, in practice, the alternative would have worked out in much the same way as the management proposal. However, this overlooks the fact that the number of *forced* redundancies under S1 was more than twice as high as under the union plan. In addition and even more importantly, in the union proposal the forced redundancies were to be spread over a period of one and a half years while under S1 the management had the power to implement them whenever natural wastage, severance payments and early retirement did not yield the desired results. Here, the decision of the supervisory board did indeed make a difference for the union, and in this respect the efforts of the union and, in particular, of the works council to turn the decision round appear entirely credible.

The new car boom
On the day after the supervisory board decision, the governments in Bonn and Hannover announced regional labour market programmes to ease the expected unemployment, especially in the Wolfsburg and the Salzgitter areas. The measures, however, did not become necessary. In

April, sales at Volkswagen began to pick up, and production was increased. In June, the severance payments programme was discontinued because in some places a manpower shortage began to be felt. (The early retirement scheme, under the pressure of the works council, remained in effect and is still operative now; Volkswagen workers today retire at age 59, with the company making up the difference in their pensions). By the end of August, the current workforce could not meet the increased demand for cars and the management in Emden and in Wolfsburg had to ask the respective works councils for overtime. Although this was granted,[9] by mid-October the recruitment ban, as far as it applied to blue-collar workers, had to be lifted. (For white-collar workers, the ban remained in effect.) On October 28, the central works council agreed to the employment of 5,000 new workers in the following eight months. In exchange, the management had to give assurance that there would be no forced dismissals in 1976, except for the disciplinary reasons under the company framework agreement. With this, S1 had been finally scrapped. Also, the management had to agree that short-time work, if it should again become necessary in the future, would take place no earlier than three months after the last overtime shift.

From mid-1975 until the end of the 1970s, Volkswagen experienced one of the strongest boom periods of its history. The number of German-built Volkswagens sold in 1976 exceeded by no less than 25.5 per cent the number sold in the year before, and sales revenue increased by 48.8 per cent. Also in 1976, profits reached DM 789 million, compared to a loss of DM 145 million in 1975. For the first time in three years, the company could afford to pay a dividend (Table 5.2). This upward trend continued for several more years. The situation at Audi NSU was similar, although the data are less easily available because of the progressive merger of the firm into Volkswagen AG (from 1976 onwards, part of the Audi NSU production was sold under the Volkswagen label).[10]

The consequences of the S1 decision

The speed with which S1 took effect took both the union and the management by surprise. Many more workers than expected accepted the severance payments and left the company. For the union, this was all the more surprising since unemployment at that time was increasing. One explanation was that workers had lost confidence in the company's future. The possibility of 10,000 forced redundancies was seen by many as a very real and very personal threat. The spreading climate of pessimism, which was in striking contrast to the traditional attitude of Volkswagen workers towards their company, was so pervasive that it was virtually unshaken by the indications during the spring of a new boom. In fact, if the union, and in a way also the management, made one mistake in the period before the decision, it was that they underestimated the psychological effect of, and the amount of anxiety brought about by, the envisaged 10,000 forced redundancies.

On the other hand, the decline of the workforce at Volkswagen would have been less rapid had the workers not had alternative employment opportunities. In this respect, the surprise of the union and the works council in particular was considerable. Although general unemployment was moving towards an unprecedented five per cent, there were jobs available for almost all of the Volkswagen workers who decided to move. In fact, what happened was that Opel and Ford, or the aerospace concern MBB from Bremen, set up recruitment offices at Wolfsburg and other locations of Volkswagen plants to persuade Volkswagen workers, especially those of foreign nationality, to take the severance payment and move to them. In some instances, complete crews of experienced operators gave up their jobs on a Friday afternoon and were taken during the weekend to their new place of employment, leaving their former employer without a chance to organise a replacement for the coming week.

While this would have upset production even in normal circumstances, at the beginning of a new boom the consequences were catastrophic. In some plants on some days, the foremen just did not know how to man the assembly line or to get their equipment repaired. Interruptions because of labour shortages were frequent. As demand continued to increase, the company soon had to extend its delivery dates; economically, this meant lower sales and a costly delay in the process of recovery. Even the discontinuation of the severance payments programme in June did not help much because it did not bring back the workers already lost. Labour shortages were particularly pronounced among the skilled workers who were necessary for efficient operation and, at least in the short run, almost impossible to replace. By mid-1975, the company found itself in a situation in which, as a result of its own manpower policy, its work-force was quantitatively and qualitatively so inadequate that most of the new opportunities offered by the market had to be left unexploited.

How strong the effect of S1 on the size and composition of the workforce at Volkswagen was can be seen from some global statistics. By April 1975, Volkswagen (excluding Audi NSU) employed 105,480 workers – 5.4 per cent fewer than at the end of 1974. In spite of the withdrawal of the severance payments offer in June and the lifting of the recruitment ban in November, employment at the end of 1975 was almost 12 per cent lower than in April, and 16.6 per cent below the level of end-1974 (Table 5.3). In fact, the scheme was so effective that although it was to run for a period of two years until the end of 1976, the difference between the size of the workforce by end-1975 – half a year after the economic situation had turned around – and the overall employment goal under S1 was only 5.7 per cent (Table 5.5).

Table 5.5　Actual Employment Compared to SI Targets, 1975 and 1976

	Differences by end of 1975, (per cent of SI target)	Differences by end of 1976, (per cent of SI target)
Volkswagen	5.7	10.7
Wolfsburg	7.8	14.3
Hannover	0.6	3.0
Braunschweig	0.0	6.1
Kassel	7.0	8.6
Emden	13.0	20.4
Salzgitter	0.0	5.7
Audi NSU	10.4	20.4
Total	6.6	12.6

Another, perhaps more adequate way of determining the effect of S1 is to compare the actual employment in October 1975 with the employment level that should have been reached under S1 at that time provided that the reduction in the workforce had been equally spread over the two year period. This is shown in Table 5.6

It is small wonder, then, that the company's wage bill in 1975 was

Table 5.6　Employment in October 1975 – Planned and Actual

	Employment in October 1975	SI target for October 1975	Per cent difference
Wolfsburg	45,000	44,350	+3.7
Hannover	17,000	17,350	−2.0
Braunschweig	5,000	5,100	−2.0
Kassel	13,800	13,800	—
Emden	6,100	5,550	+9.9
Salzgitter	5,300	6,050	−12.4
Total for Volkswagen	93,200	92,200	+1.1

DM 347 million or 8.8 per cent lower than in 1974; this was the main reason for the decrease in the losses from DM 555 million in 1974 to DM 145 million in 1975 (Table 5.2).

The development at Audi NSU was different. Here, too, the decline in employment accelerated sharply after April 1975. Between end-1974 and the supervisory board decision on S1, employment fell by 4.8 per cent. In the following eight months, employment fell by 15.3 per cent. However, while the workforce during the whole of 1975 was reduced by 19.4 per cent – which was more than at Volkswagen – at the end of the year it was still 10.4 per cent above the S1 goal (Table 5.5). In the following year, 1976, employment at Audi NSU increased by no less than 9 per cent, while at Volkswagen the increase was only 4.7 per cent.

Comparison of the employment figures at the end of 1975 and 1976 with the S1 targets, shows that in three Volkswagen plants – Hannover, Braunschweig and Salzgitter – the targets set for the end of 1976 had already been reached by December 1975 (Table 5.5). In the other three plants, employment was well above the S1 level, most clearly in Emden where the difference was 13 per cent. The expansion of employment in 1976 benefited primarily Wolfsburg and Emden, while Hannover, Salzgitter and Braunschweig still remained relatively close to their S1 goals.

Other consequences of the S1 plan relate to the internal composition of the workforce (Table 5.3). Here, the trends already observed in 1974 continued. The number of foreign workers again declined by about 6,500 and their number was almost halved.[11] Also above average was the decline in the number of female workers (– 23 per cent) and blue-collar workers in general (– 18 per cent). On the other hand, unlike 1974 the white-collar workforce was also reduced, if only by 1,100. The average age continued to increase, and so did the average length of service.

Aftermath

With hindsight, the IGM and the Volkswagen works council feel that their reactions to the 1975 crisis were appropriate and correct. Both see the events before and after the supervisory board decision as a demonstration that co-determination does not interfere with 'economic necessities', and that a company under co-determination can weather a major economic crisis without having to rely on public subsidies. In this respect, the history of the S1 scheme is seen as confirming a point, often made by the unions, which, in their view, is not sufficiently appreciated by the public. Although the behaviour of IGM at Volkswagen had no visible impact on the then pending legislation on extended co-determination – which was watered down in spite of it – many unionists still believe that the example of co-operative crisis management given at

Volkswagen was, and still is, politically useful for them.

As to IGM in particular, there was in the second half of 1975 a strong sense of pride among headquarters officials that they had predicted the market more accurately than the management of a company as big as Volkswagen. This feeling was quite independent of the fact that at the time there had been considerable internal uncertainty as to the validity of the adopted position. The sense of triumph prevailing at IGM was reinforced by Schmücker himself who several times professed publicly that his pessimistic expectations had been wrong and that the union analysis of the situation had been more realistic. In fact, there are newspaper accounts of Loderer jokingly reminding Schmücker that he had better listen to the union if he wanted to make a profit, and of Schmücker responding in the same vein that Volkswagen would indeed be so much better off if the management had only listened to Loderer in time.

Another reason why the 1975 events were viewed so euphorically by the IGM in retrospect seems to have been that the political risks the crisis had presented to the union had not materialised. The central political problem the IGM had to solve at Volkswagen was how to act as an industrial union – in accordance with the political imperatives of equally representing the interests of all workers in a large and hetrogeneous industry – without losing the confidence of, and the control over, the workforce at Volkswagen. From the beginning, the IGM and Loderer in particular, had been resolved to fight whatever tendency there may have been to sacrifice NSU in favour of higher job security at Volkswagen. Also, they had been aware that they could not go out for government subsidies to pay the high Volkswagen wages because, among other things, their other members would not in the long term have stood for this. If it wanted to survive as an industrial union, IGM had to accept the premise that job security at Volkswagen could be restored only by restoring profitability, even if this required that a major part of the workforce had to be made redundant. For IGM, the 1975 events were proof that this position could be made plausible to the members.

As far as the Volkswagen works council is concerned, the 1975 crisis represented a dramatic experience which changed its attitudes to manpower policy. S1 was the first occasion on which the works council was confronted with the perspective of large-scale redundancies in a time of general economic stagnation. The 1972 lay-off, and to some extent even the considerable employment reduction of 1974, had been given much less attention and had caused much less anxiety among both works councillors and workers. The new significance of manpower policy for the works council was reflected in the management's decision to present S1 to the supervisory board rather than putting it in effect on its own – a move which, as will be seen in the following case study, set an important precedent for the conduct of manpower policy at Volkswagen in the future. Apart from this procedural aspect, the substantive effect of the 1975 events was that they led the works council to place more emphasis than before on the notion of 'steady employment' – in particular, to call for co-operative manpower planning as a means of smoothing out the employment cycle and making the size of the workforce as independent of the development of the product market as possible.

Footnotes

[1] The same development is reflected in a comparison, also made by IGM, of the ratio of sales per employee at Volkswagen and at other major German car producers. Whereas at Daimler-Benz the ratio between 1968 and 1973 increased by 67 per cent and at Ford and Opel by 63 and 49 per cent respectively, at Volkswagen the increase was no higher than 15 per cent.

[2] For example, the VW411, the VW1600, the VW-Porsche 914, the K70 and the RO80.

[3] In June and July – 3,480; in October, November and December – 3,920.

[4] The Volkswagen wage agreement of the crisis year of 1974 (the result of arbitration) provided for a general wage increase of 11 per cent taking effect in February and for an additional increase of 2 per cent in December. In addition, holidays were increased by two days a year, the holiday bonus was raised from 30 to 50 per cent of a month's pay and an additional Christmas bonus of DM 250 for each employee was introduced on top of the existing Christmas bonus which was the equivalent of a full month's pay.

[5] The only strike at Volkswagen and Audi NSU during the period under study seems to have been an unofficial walk-out at the Wolfsburg plant in the spring of 1973. As far as it is possible to ascertain, the dispute was unrelated to redundancy problems. It lasted only a few hours.

[6] Insofar as the moderation of the IGM during the Volkswagen crisis was aimed at strengthening the Social-Democratic position on the co-determination Bill, it was not successful. At the instigation of the Free Democrats, the Bill was watered down during the Bundestag deliberations to such an extent that at the end many unions felt it would have been preferable if it had not been passed.

[7] Another way in which a 'responsible' attitude was forced upon the union was its easy access to the government and, in particular, to the Chancellor. On various occasions during the crisis, Loderer met Schmidt to talk about the situation at Volkswagen. Most of these meetings took place at Schmidt's invitation; officially, they were to give the Chancellor an opportunity to ask for advice in handling the crisis. Being asked in this way, however, as one of Loderer's advisers put it in an interview, 'you cannot afford just to say nothing or to talk nonsense. You have to offer something realistic.'

[8] There were even rumours in the press that in February the company had difficulty in financing its payroll.

[9] In the remaining four months of the year, overtime shifts were worked in Wolfsburg and Emden by 12,000 workers on 14 consecutive Saturdays.

[10] The two components of Audi NSU have to be looked at separately. While

Audi in Ingolstadt throughout the period was in better condition than all other plants of the Volkswagen concern, the problems accumulated at NSU. Although NSU as a result of IGM pressure was not closed completely, one smaller plant (Hohenstein) was shut. The 470 workers were either transferred to Audi or other Volkswagen plants or went to Daimler-Benz in Stuttgart. The main NSU plant, Neckarsulm, had to switch to one-shift operation and its workforce was reduced almost to the level envisaged in the S1 scheme. The plant now produces two of the larger Audi models. Also, Neckarsulm, by way of a job order, assembles a new Porsche model for which Porsche itself has not enough capacity.

[11] At Audi NSU, the foreign workforce was reduced from 24.1 to 16.2 per cent. Although this was a significant decline, the percentage of foreign workers remained considerably above the level at Volkswagen – see Table 5.3).

6   The Volkswagen Assembly Plant in the United States

One cause of the Volkswagen crisis in the early 1970s was the company's declining sales in the United States. The last year in which the number of Volkswagens sold in America increased was 1970. From then on, the continuing fall of the dollar against the mark was accompanied by a similarly rapid drop of Volkswagen sales in America. In 1974, when the dollar had fallen to DM 2.59 (Table 6.1), Volkswagen sold only 334,000 cars in the United States – which was about 30 per cent fewer than in the year before – and allegedly lost DM 200 million on its American operations. At this point, the management for the first time publicly called for a Volkswagen plant in the United States as a way of becoming independent of the fluctuations in the value of the dollar. Although such plans had been floated since about 1972, it was only in June of 1974 – when Volkswagen was faced with the prospect of having to give up the American market altogether – that the then managing director, Leiding, officially informed the company's decision-making bodies of plans to produce in the United States.

In the following years, Volkswagen sales in the United States continued to decline, and the losses, by all accounts, continued to grow. Although Volkswagen sold its cars in America at such a low price that American car producers started legal action under the anti-dumping laws, the number of cars sold went down in 1975 by another 17 per cent. Meanwhile, the American small cars market, which had for years been dominated by Volkswagen, was taken over by the Japanese. The only reason why Volkswagen continued to export cars to the United States by the mid-1970s was to keep its American dealers' organisation together. Even this goal, however, was becoming increasingly difficult to achieve. From about 1972, Volkswagen dealers in the United States, in order to remain in business, had begun to sell other cars also – mainly Japanese. This development was accelerated when in 1975 Volkswagen, because of the high losses it made on cars sold in America, limited its supply to its American dealers. It was in this situation that, on 23 April 1976, the Volkswagen supervisory board unanimously approved the proposal by the Schmücker management board to set up a Volkswagen assembly plant in the United States. The following account describes the position taken by the IGM and the Volkswagen works council on this issue, and analyses the role of co-determination in

Table 6.1   *Deutsche Mark/Dollar Exchange Rate*

	Deutsche Mark per Dollar	Rate of change (per cent)
1969	4.00	
1970	3.65	−8.8
1971	3.48	−4.7
1972	3.19	−8.3
1973	2.66	−16.6
1974	2.59	−2.6
1975	2.46	−5.0

the resolution of the conflicts of interests between workers and management on investment in a foreign country.

The multinational strategy

The decline in value of the US dollar was not the only cause of Volkswagen's losses on the American market. As pointed out in an article by one of IGM's car industry experts in the union journal in early 1976, the overall trade surplus of the West German economy in spite of the changes in the international monetary system, had not declined after 1969 but, on the contrary, considerably increased (from DM 16 billion in 1970 to DM 37 billion in 1975). This indicated that most German exporting firms had been well able to adapt to the new exchange rates. The reason why Volkswagen had not was, according to the article, its poor performance in productivity. The author concluded that Volkswagen's declining competitiveness in the United States, and the need to transfer production to North America, was not primarily due to the monetary situation but to poor management.

It is interesting to note that this line of reasoning was never publicly adopted by the IGM leadership. Under co-determination, productivity is not solely a matter for the management but, at least *de facto*, also one for the union. A union which has the institutional power to make management efforts to raise productivity fail, cannot complain about low productivity without laying itself open to management demands for co-operation in doing something about it. Both the management and the union at Volkswagen were aware of the need to improve productivity and were in fact holding talks about it at that time. However, there were good reasons for both sides to keep these talks as much behind closed doors as possible − not only to protect their mutual relations from deteriorating but also to preserve their bargaining positions. It was because of such considerations that the attempt by one of their expert staff to play up the productivity issue was not welcomed by the IGM leadership.

Another cause of Volkswagen's declining competitiveness in America was the high Volkswagen wages. In 1975, wages at Volkswagen were about 5 per cent higher than at other German car producers, and about 10 per cent above the average of the German engineering industry. In 1970, the differential between Volkswagen wage rates and the rest of the engineering industry had been as much as 23 per cent. What was more important was that under the new exchange rates, Volkswagen wages by the mid-1970s exceeded the wage level in the American car industry. Whereas in 1970 average labour costs per hour in the American car industry, including fringe benefits and social security contributions, had been equivalent to DM 19.60, in 1975 they had declined, at the current exchange rate, to DM 18.70. At Volkswagen, by way of comparison, labour costs per hour increased during the same period from DM 11.20 to DM 19.59. In other words, while in 1970 the average hourly wage at Volkswagen was equal to 57.1 per cent of the average in the American car industry, in 1975 it was as high as 104.3 per cent. In addition there was the fact that because of fewer holidays and shorter vacations, American car workers worked about 30 to 40 days per year more than their German counterparts. These differences provided the management with strong arguments in favour of transferring production for the American market to the United States, and they obviously did not fail to impress the union to whose efforts the high wage level in Germany was at least partly due.

The role of wage differentials puts the decision on the US plant into the general context of Volkswagen's development since the 1960s into a multinational company. While there may have been very special reasons for transferring production to the United States (for example, the transport costs from Germany which in 1976 were as high as DM 400 per car; the frequent strikes in the East Coast sea ports during which cars had to be rerouted to the West Coast; the need to become independent of the shaky dollar), this was not the first time that Volkswagen had set up a plant in a foreign country. The events in the first half of the 1970s served only to accelerate a process which had been under way for a considerable time. In 1970, Volkswagen had three foreign subsidiaries – one each in Brazil, Mexico and South Africa[1] which produced 12.5 per cent of the company's total output (Table 6.2). By 1976, this percentage had risen to 33.7 – almost three times as much as six years before. The highest increases took place in 1972 (from 15.1 to 23.7 per cent) when domestic production declined by 16.3 per cent whereas foreign production went up by 46.1 per cent, and in 1974 (from 26.3 to 34.3 per cent) with domestic production going down by 21 per cent and foreign production rising by 15.3 per cent. Had it not been for the foreign subsidiaries, the Volkswagen crisis after 1970 would have been even more serious.

Table 6.2   Volkswagen International(a) Production

Year	Total number of cars produced (000s)			German production (per cent)
	Worldwide	Abroad	Germany	
1970	2,215	277	1,938	87.5
1971	2,354	356	1,998	84.9
1972	2,193	520	1,672	76.3
1973	2,335	615	1,720	73.3
1974	2,068	709	1,359	65.7
1975	1,949	720	1,229	63.1
1976	2,166	730	1,436	66.3

(a) Including Audi NSU and foreign subsidiaries

One of the main aspects, then, of the crisis the company went through in the early 1970s was that during its course, quite apart from the plans for a plant in the United States, Volkswagen became increasingly multinational. Just as the decline of domestic production was accompanied by a growth of foreign production, the cutback on employment in Germany coincided with an increase in employment abroad. While in 1970 only 18 per cent of the total Volkswagen workforce were employed by the foreign subsidiaries, in 1976 this proportion had increased to 32 per cent. Whatever factors may also have played a role, this reflected a general tendency of car producers to become multinational companies: to react to rising wage costs in the industrialised countries, and to changes in the world car market, by transferring production to countries with lower wages and less saturated markets. It was against this general background that the plans of the Volkswagen management to set up a plant in the United States had to be assessed by the IGM.

The union attitude
Since the late 1960s, the IGM and the works council had warned against Volkswagen's increasing dependence on the US market and on the dollar. When the crisis occurred, however, they agreed with the management that the company's American market share had to be defended as far as possible. While for the management this appeared necessary to regain profitability, the main consideration for the union and the works council was to protect the jobs of workers in the German plants. In early 1976, about 16,000 Volkswagen workers in Germany were working for export to the United States. Giving up or losing the US market would have meant that, other things being equal, these workers would have lost their jobs. On the other hand, what made the position of the union

more difficult than that of the management was that recovering the US market by transferring production to the United States could have had, from the viewpoint of these workers, exactly the same effect: while it would have solved the problem of profitability, it could nevertheless have destroyed their jobs.

The IGM does not in principle oppose foreign investment by German firms. German industrial unions are generally well aware of the fact that it is largely as a result of their own successes that firms may have to transfer production to countries with lower wages. In this respect, unions in advanced industrialised countries are faced with a basic strategic dilemma: by increasing real wages, they may undermine their equally important goal of secure employment. On the other hand, since a firm's capacity to pay high wages depends on its profitability, foreign investment to the extent that it protects profitability is not always in contradiction to union interests. In so far as foreign investment is a reaction to high domestic labour costs, it may in the long run be counterproductive for unions to prevent it in the name of employment security. In export-oriented industries, production in foreign countries may be the only way for a firm to remain competitive. Competitiveness, however, is the main precondition not only for high wages but also for secure employment.

From the perspective of trade unions, the central aspect of a transfer of production to a foreign country is its likely effect on the domestic labour market. One possibility is that the creation of new jobs abroad will reduce the number of jobs at home. It is also possible, however, that investment will result in higher sales and thus create additional jobs. In both cases, the transfer of production to foreign countries means the export of jobs. But while in the first instance the jobs exported are those of workers already employed, in the second they may be additional jobs to which nobody can presently make a claim. It is obvious that the latter kind of job export is much more acceptable to a trade union than the former. In so far as a management can show that a planned transfer of production will not reduce the existing workforce but will be at the expense of those who may in the future apply for employment, it stands a good chance of getting union support. An analogous case is natural wastage as an instrument of manpower reduction which also safeguards the interests of the present workforce by reducing the employment opportunities of people not presently in the organisation. Managements proposing natural wastage to reduce employment usually find it relatively easy to get unions to co-operate.

It is characteristic of the IGM's general attitude, and of the 'responsible' style of trade unionism fostered by co-determination, that the union never perceived the US plant project simply as a matter of 'jobs versus profits'. Once the plan had been brought up by the management, the IGM was very careful to discuss it strictly 'on its merits'. From the beginning, the union leadership did not preclude the possibility that there were indeed good economic reasons, including those relating to employment, for some kind of a Volkswagen venture in the United States. In fact, the conclusion at which the leadership and their experts seem to have arrived relatively soon was that although a transfer of production to America might put some domestic jobs in peril, not doing so would in the long run endanger even more jobs.

Nevertheless, the proposal by the Volkswagen management to produce in the United States confronted the union with complex technical problems and difficult choices. In a sense, the US plant project created a conflict not so much between union and management but rather between the union's short-term and long-term interests. What the union had to discuss with the management was not the relatively simple question of whether there should be foreign investment and 'job export' or not; rather, the problem was the much more difficult one of how many and what kind of jobs should be 'exported' and when. To protect the long-term interests of its members, the union had to permit as many jobs to be transferred to America as were necessary for the company to recover its competitiveness on the American market, and it had to press for as many jobs to be kept in Germany as possible without making Volkswagen's American operations unprofitable. With an optimal work sharing between the new American plant and the existing plants in Germany, there was even the possibility that as a result of increasing sales in the United States, the number of workers producing in Germany for the US market would soon be as high as before the establishment of the US plant. On the other hand, it could not be ruled out that, if only in the short run, some workers might lose their jobs or suffer in other ways from the US project. To the extent that there was in this sense a possibility of 'job export', the union had to defend as credibly and as successfully as possible the interests of the workers affected, if only to remain politically able to defend the long term interests of the workforce as well. In other words, the strategic task for the IGM was to try to influence in detail the impending decision on the kind and the size of the US plant, its relationship with the German plants, and the timing of its getting into operation while at the same time, in exchange for its agreement to the project as such, fighting for a maximum of protection for the existing workforce without thereby prejudicing the success of the US plant or the economic recovery of the company as a whole.

Union and works council
The formulation of a joint policy on the part of the workers' representatives was complicated by the fact that union and works council tended

to emphasise different aspects of the interests of their common constituency. While the works council was aware of the need to restore the long-term economic viability of the company, it was under pressure from the workforce to prevent any export of jobs, however short-term, to the United States. The IGM leadership, on the other hand, while recognising its members' short-term interests, was far enough removed from the shop floor to see the problem primarily in a long-term perspective. The resulting conflict was most serious at Emden which at that time produced exclusively for the American market and where almost no alternative employment opportunities existed.

When the US project was under consideration, the Emden works council was confronted with opposition by various communist groups inside and outside the workforce – and even inside the IGM *Vertrauenskörper* – which attacked the works council and the union for an alleged lack of determination in protecting the Emden workers' jobs. This made it politically necessary for the works council to emphasise its independence of both the IGM headquarters and the central works council. While in other plants the issue was less prominent, it was still explosive enough for the works councils to move carefully and not to identify themselves too closely with the more general and long-term perspective of the union. For the union and the central works council, this meant that if they wanted to develop a united position of all workers' representatives at Volkswagen, they had to be prepared for a lengthy period of careful and patient internal negotiating.

Because of the considerable political risks that were involved, it was incumbent upon Loderer himself to take the lead in this process. Whether or not he could be successful depended largely on what the management and the shareholders were prepared to concede in exchange for the union's final assent. In effect, the union leadership thus faced the precarious task of having to negotiate with, and in a sense to mediate between, two partners with opposite perspectives: with the various works councils and *Vertrauenskörper* who tended to oppose the project, and with the management which was strongly in favour of it.

The situation on the supervisory board
Under German law, investment decisions of the dimension of the Volkswagen US plant require approval by the supervisory board. The procedure is that the management prepares a detailed plan and asks the supervisory board for its assent. As in the case of the S1 scheme, therefore, the composition of the supervisory board and the relative power of its members were crucial factors for the union in devising its strategy on the US project. Obviously, the private shareholders were prepared to support a US plant, although there was a possibility of disagreement among them on the specifics. Also generally in favour was

the Federal government which not only was interested in the company's economic recovery but also welcomed the effects which a transfer of production to the United States might be expected to have on the balance of trade and payments. The situation was different with the Land of Niedersachsen where all major Volkswagen plants, including Emden, are located. For the Land, the primary concern was to prevent regional unemployment. In this respect, it came very close to the position of the Volkswagen local works councils.

Thus, while many factors were hard to assess beforehand – for example, the final attitude of the Federal government which in this instance might not have mustered the political strength to be unresponsive to the union, there were good reasons for the management to adopt a consensual approach and to try to negotiate with the union informally and in advance of the supervisory board vote, a solution which both sides could accept.

1974: The Leiding project

The first time the Volkswagen management officially stated its intention to set up a plant in the United States was in mid-1974 – shortly before the end of the Leiding era. The way Leiding handled the US project contributed to his demise. While plans to produce in the US existed before 1974, originally they were kept secret, and the management was ordered by the managing director not to talk about them to the union. When the project leaked out anyway, the union's inevitable suspicions were increased by the initial secrecy. The consequent negative reaction of the union in turn discouraged the management and slowed the project down further. It is true – as the IGM later emphasised on various occasions in public statements – that the union never vetoed Leiding's US plans, and that it could not have done so because it was never formally presented with them.[2] This, however, was largely because Leiding realised that he would be unable to persuade the union to support the project. 'Co-operative' unionism presupposes co-operative management; if a management is not prepared to give the union an opportunity to influence decisions at an early stage, the union is forced into a reactive, defensive, and in this sense 'negative', position. Obtaining co-operation, from the perspective of management, requires avoidance of unilateral action and, at least to some extent, power-sharing. In this sense, co-operative labour relations are no doubt costly for the management. But if the union is strong – for instance, if it is an industrial union unchallenged by inter-union competition – non-co-operation can be even more costly because it is likely to result in deadlock. The more a management insists on preserving its 'autonomy', the more it may lose control over the course of events.

One of the reasons why the Leiding project was doomed to fail was that it had been developed without any prior consultation with the union and the works council. The management is not legally obliged to have such consultations, but neither is the union obliged to support an investment decision of which it first hears in the press. Advance consultations would have given the management an impression of the union's attitudes and of the political constraints under which the union had to act. In such consultations, the IGM would undoubtedly have let the management know that 1974 – when the Volkswagen crisis was at its peak – was not the appropriate time to talk about a new Volkswagen plant abroad. This was even more pertinent since the Leiding proposal, as it became public in 1974, involved the building of a complete, integrated production plant which would have made a step-by-step transition from German to American production impossible. Without a gradual 'phasing in' of the American operation, a negative employment effect in Germany would not only have been inevitable but would have occurred at once rather than being spread over a longer period. Since this was unacceptable from the perspective of the workers, the Leiding proposal stood no chance of getting union or works council support.

There were other objections as well which were shared not only by the union but also by some of the private shareholders and even by members of the Volskwagen top management. Building a completely new car factory abroad required considerable investment which would have been difficult to finance even in normal times. In 1974, however, Volkswagen already had high investment needs because of the model change, and there was no way of predicting when the company would start to make profits again. The way the Leiding project was laid out, it presented a tremendous economic risk. If the US plant – which according to IGM estimates would have cost as much as DM 3,000 million – had failed, the company as a whole could easily have become bankrupt. It was not only to the union that this prospect appeared disturbing. When the union criticised the Leiding project in public for being 'oversized', it was well aware that it spoke not only on behalf of its members but also of some of the shareholders.

1975–76: The Schmücker approach

One of the first decisions Schmücker made when he took office was to disentangle the manpower reduction problem from the problem of the US project. This was not because the latter had become any less urgent economically. By dealing with one problem at a time, however, and by postponing the US project until after the implementation of S1, the management made it easier for the union to adopt a 'responsible' position on both issues. Although during the negotiations on S1 the US project was, according to a senior IGM official in an interview, 'always on everybody's mind', the point was that for the public the two issues became separated, and that in particular the US plant could now be decided after the exact size and the consequences of the domestic employment reduction were known. Also, the new schedule made it possible for the management, in dealing with the US investment problem, to draw on the confidence established between itself and the union during the S1 negotiations. In this sense, the delay of the US investment decision may not even have been a loss of time – especially since the management used the rest of 1975 for a careful screening of possible production sites in America and for developing a number of alternative scenarios to be discussed later with the union.

By early 1976, Volkswagen's problems on the American market had grown to such a dimension that action could no longer be deferred. In April, the Rabbit sold in the United States for $3,499. Although at this price the company made heavy losses, in the same month the Honda Civic was sold for $2,729, the Toyota Corolla for $2,789, the AMC Gremlin for $2,889, and the Ford Pinto for $2,976. It is not surprising, then, that in the first two months of the year, Volkswagen sales in America were 43 per cent below the level of the year before. Under the impact of this catastrophic decline, the dealers' network – which had been built up over long years with considerable investment – began to disintegrate. While in late 1973 there had been 1,200 Volkswagen dealers in the US, in early 1976 their number had fallen to about 1,100, of which 600 were also selling Japanese cars. At this stage, it was clear to both the management and the union that if the American market was not to be totally lost, a decision had to be made fast – if only to re-assure the dealers and to persuade them not to give up Volkswagen completely.

Union and works council: internal consensus building
It has been said that in principle the IGM leadership recognised the need for Volkswagen to invest in the United States and was prepared, in certain conditions, to give the project its support. After the S1 scheme had been accepted by the supervisory board, Loderer indicated in several interviews with the press that a unanimous decision was possible on the US plant provided that the management made a number of concessions. One political reason for this attitude was that the union wanted to avoid being outvoted on the supervisory board for a second time. Another was the ongoing public debate on co-determination. Just as the strong position of the IGM at Volkswagen had been blamed for the company's over-sized workforce and high wages, it was now held responsible by conservative journalists and politicians for the fact that Volkswagen did not already have an American plant. Since the IGM did not want this to continue, it was interested in bringing the US plant issue to a fast and, above all, consensual solution.

To make this possible, the IGM leadership had to develop a policy which could be supported by the central works council and all local works councils alike. The main stumbling block in this turned out to be Emden. There was obviously no way of getting the Emden works council to support a positive vote on the supervisory board if Emden was to be closed down. In many ways, there were parallels here with Neckarsulm under the SI scheme: without an equitable distribution of the inevitable sacrifices among all groups of affected members, an industrial union is not able to support industrial change, however economically necessary it may be. In the present case, 'equity' did not just mean that Emden remained in operation. In an early phase of the informal negotiations between union and management, there was a plan to change over at Emden, just as at Neckarsulm the year before, to one-shift operation, thereby reducing the workforce by a half. This was declared unacceptable by the Emden works council which, because of its problems with its left-wing opponents, was in a far better position internally than the works council of NSU in 1974. When Emden rejected the one-shift proposal, therefore, the IGM and the central works council had to go back to the management and persuade it to come up with a better offer.

In December 1975, after the recruitment ban at Volkswagen had been lifted, the union leadership felt that the time was right to tackle the matter head-on. To prepare for the impending decision, a meeting of all members of the Volkswagen local and central works councils – altogether about 120 people – was convened at the head office in Frankfurt. The discussion, according to a participant, was heated, and no consensus was reached. In February of 1976, another meeting of the same circle was called for 18 March in Hannover. Meanwhile, the informal negotiations between union and management continued. Shortly before the second meeting, on 28 February, Loderer in a newspaper interview for the first time advocated the US project in public. He also specified some of the conditions upon which he thought the union's assent should depend. The discussion of the works councillors in Hannover was again controversial. This time, however, the leadership prevailed. No formal vote was taken, but 'at the end of the day it was clear that the majority gave the US plant their reluctant approval' (Interview). After the meeting, Loderer, according to interview information, 'had by and large a free hand' with regard to the project. A few days later, the Volkswagen management board met with the central works council. Here, in Loderer's absence, the opponents of the plant made their last attempt to prevent it. After they had failed, all works councillors and most of the *Vertrauensleute* – the significant exception being sections of the *Vertrauenskörper* at Emden – supported the IGM official position.

Loderer's press interview of 28 February is a highly instructive document, and there is no doubt that it contributed to bringing about the result obtained at the meeting two weeks later. To begin with, Loderer stated that because of the competition on the American market, a fast and positive decision on the US project was necessary. The union, he argued, had in the past criticised the management for making the economic wellbeing of the company overly dependent upon the US dollar; consequently, it could not in principle oppose the project. He also emphasised that it was only the dollar problem, and not the allegedly excessive wages at Volkswagen, which made the US plant necessary. Loderer attributed the fact that there was no Volkswagen plant in the US yet, to Leiding and his habit of 'ignoring the works council'. With Schmücker's succession, the conditions for an agreement had improved: 'I understand that the management now seeks a unanimous decision of the supervisory board'. Also, Loderer defended the initial reluctance of the union to agree to the project by saying that the required investment was 'so large that too much caution is better than too little'. As to the conditions under which the union would be prepared to agree, Loderer first stated that closing down Emden was possible 'only over my dead body'. In addition he demanded a long-term manpower policy by which to protect the jobs of the presently employed workforce, and a ban on the import of American-produced Volkswagens to Germany and other European countries. Asked about the alleged 'productivity problem' at Volkswagen, Loderer answered that this 'will have to be carefully studied as to its causes'. If it should turn out that such a problem in fact existed, the union was prepared 'to do something about it in co-operation with the management'.[3]

Favourable circumstances
Early in 1976, employment in the German Volkswagen plants, as a result of the SI policy, was at an all-time low. At the same time, sales continued to go up – as they had been doing for months – and the prospect of a new Volkswagen boom was becoming more probable. This situation was quite different from that in 1974 when Leiding was about to launch his US project. It is much easier for a union to agree to investment abroad when demand is expanding and the domestic workforce is small. On the other hand, setting up a production plant and getting it into operation takes time. If the decision to produce in a foreign country is made in the early phase of a boom, it is possible that the new plant will begin production in a period of market contraction. In this case, domestic employment may be seriously hurt – much more seriously than if the decision had been made at a time of market decline. However, while leading IGM officials were well aware of this – and in fact believed it would be more rational from the perspective of steady

employment to decide about foreign investment during a cyclical contraction period – they knew that the more rational approach was not feasible politically, and that to arrive at a decision at all they had to content themselves with a less than fully rational solution.

There were two factors in early 1976 which made it easier for IGM to agree to the US plant. The first was the conservative employment policy adopted by the management and the works council at Volkswagen after mid-1975. (This policy, which was referred to by its defenders as 'middle-line employment policy,' is described in more detail in the next chapter.) When in May of 1975 demand for Volkswagen cars began to increase again, the company deferred taking on new workers for as long as possible. Instead they tried to satisfy the additional demand by increasing the amount of overtime worked. Although, at the end of the year, this was no longer feasible and new workers had to be taken on, both management and works councils remained anxious to employ only as many new workers as absolutely necessary. This attitude, which prevailed until the late 1970s, was partly a result of the S1 experience which neither the works council nor the management wanted to go through again. It also was to do with the impending decision on the US plant. In principle, the smaller the domestic Volkswagen workforce was kept in advance of the US plant going into operation, the fewer jobs would be threatened in Germany by the transfer of production. Similarly, a relatively small workforce would make it easier for the management during the negotiations on the project to concede some kind of an 'employment guarantee' for the existing workforce and this would mean less opposition for the union to overcome internally in agreeing to the project. In these respects, the S1 policy, and the fact that it had been so effective in such a short time, had created advantages which neither side wanted to give up lightly and for the preservation of which both were prepared to pay a high price. For the company, this price consisted of longer delivery terms – which were economically risky because Volkswagen in the past had been renowned for its short dates of delivery – and an estimated loss of sales in 1976 of about 10,000 cars which could not be built because of the undersized workforce. For the works council and, in particular, for the union – which in anticipation of the US project supported the works council's participation in Volkswagen's new employment policy[4] – the price was internal political conflicts on the proper employment policy of an industrial union in a period of rising unemployment (see Chapter 7).

The second factor facilitating a positive decision by the union was, ironically, that the proportion of German-produced Volkswagens sold in America had so sharply decreased during recent years. While in the second half of 1975 and in early 1976 domestic sales had started to increase again, sales in America had continued to decline. The result was that, as Loderer put it in a press interview, 'fewer and fewer people at Volkswagen are working for export to the United States, and more and more for the domestic market, for France and Italy'. In this respect, the crisis of Volkswagen on the American market had contributed to creating the preconditions for its solution.

Management concessions

Under pressure from the union, and to enable the IGM leadership to persuade all relevant groups of members to go along with its decision on the US project, the management in its informal negotiations with Loderer offered a number of concessions. Some of these were primarily symbolic, but others had real substance. First and most importantly, the US plant was to be just an assembly plant. While Leiding had intended to build a complete production plant, Schmücker suggested that the labour-intensive parts of the American-made Volkswagen should be produced in Germany and shipped to the United States; the remaining parts, including the body, would be bought from American suppliers. In principle, which parts were to be produced in Germany and which in America would be negotiable between union and management. The idea was to start with a high proportion of German-made parts in order to prevent a sudden negative effect on employment in Germany and to make possible what Schmücker used to refer to as a 'soft landing' – a gradual transition to, and phasing in of, American production.

While this was much more acceptable to the union than the original Leiding plan, the concept of a flexible, and adjustable, division of work between the German plants and the American 'assembly plant' raised the problem of procedural safeguards to ensure that the union continued to be involved in further decisions on this matter. From the perspective of the management, the reduced dimension of the American investment had the advantage that it presented a smaller economic risk – the costs of the assembly plant were estimated to be about DM 400 million – and thus responded to many of the points raised by the internal opponents among the management and the shareholders. As a further concession to the union, the management offered an assurance that no American-built Volkswagens would be marketed in Europe, and that the production of the US plant would be sold only in North America.

After agreement had been reached on the reduction of the project to an assembly plant and on a ban on 're-importation', the main remaining point was the demand by the workers' representatives for some kind of a guarantee of employment – an assurance that workers in Germany would not be made redundant as a consequence of the US project. Especially against the background of the S1 experience, it was clear to the union leadership that without something of this kind an internal consensus on the project would not be possible.

During the informal negotiations, the management came up with the offer of a detailed work-sharing arrangement among the German plants, in which Emden was to be fully included. A similar solution, albeit on a smaller scale, had already been agreed upon a year before for Neckarsulm. In both instances, the most economically rational decision – closing down one entire plant – was not feasible because of union resistance. The 'suboptimal' alternative was a redistribution of work among all plants, including the one which, from a purely economic point of view, should have been closed. Making such a solution work posed much more complex management problems than straight-forward plant closure, and this is another example of how co-determination makes the tasks of management more demanding.

Specifically, the management's proposal provided for a 'plant utili-sation scheme' to be discussed between the management and the central works council with an understanding that both sides were willing to reach agreement. The result of these talks was to be presented by the managing director together with the US project to the supervisory board, and the two proposals were to be voted upon as a 'package'.

Although this offer went a long way towards meeting the demands of the union, it was obviously not the 'employment guarantee' that had been asked for by the Emden works council. In its view a more explicit commitment by the management was needed to satisfy members' expectations.[5] Thus negotiations had to continue. On 14 April, shortly before the supervisory board meeting, Loderer, in a speech at a works meeting in the Braunschweig Volkswagen plant, again publicly explained his position. A summary of the speech was distributed by the IGM press office, and it is instructive to read this document in full.

Eugen Loderer: Workers Demand Concrete Guarantees of Employment at Volkswagen

In a works meeting at Volkswagen in Braunschweig, the chairman of the IGM and vice-chairman of the Volkswagen supervisory board, Eugen Loderer, said that in a decision like the one on a Volkswagen plant in the United States, it was obvious that commercial and social interests could come into conflict. There were certain signs and tendencies, though, which gave the impression that a satisfactory compromise was not impossible.

The management, Loderer said, proceeded on the assumption that if the US project were realised, the level of employment in Germany could be maintained. On this, the IGM wanted a binding undertaking and a reliable guarantee. 'A company which is able to have a middle-range investment plan should be able to plan its manpower policy for the same period,' Loderer said. The workers were demanding more meaningful domestic manpower planning and an integrated concept of manpower policy for all German Volkswagen plants. Loderer: 'We demand that declarations of intent to this effect by the management are given a binding form, before the assembly plant in the United States goes into full operation.'

Loderer emphasised that the workers shared with the management an interest in protecting Volkswagen's American market. At the same time, however, the workers demanded that the management share their interest in protecting jobs in German plants.

Today nobody could still be in doubt, Loderer said, that the representatives of the workers on the Volkswagen supervisory board were prepared to share in the responsibility for decisions on company policy. On the other hand, nobody should be mistaken in thinking that what counted for workers' representatives was not profit guarantees for shareholders but employment guarantees for workers. The representatives of the workers would agree to financial commitments only if the management also made commitments on employment. 'A green light for investment abroad will be given by the workers' representatives only if the management at the same time gives a red light for a reduction of domestic employment', Loderer emphasised.

Although the union pressed its point vigorously, it became clear that for the management an explicit guarantee of employment was out of the question. In part, this was because nobody could rule out for certain a new major car crisis in which the company would have had to face the unpleasant alternative of either withdrawing its 'employment guarantee' or risking its economic survival. Probably even more important were the possible political effects of an employment guarantee (for example, it could set a precedent for future negotiations or for other firms and industrial sectors) and the likely adverse reactions of banks and investors. All the management felt it could concede, therefore, was a declaration not on its future decisions but on the expected, positive, development of the product market and of the company's consequent demand for labour. More specifically, the managing director was prepared to state, as part of the formal proceedings of the supervisory board, that given the present and foreseeable situation on the market and provided that nothing extraordinary happened, the management did not expect that workers would have to be dismissed as a consequence of the US project. After some internal debate, the proposal of the management taken in conjunction with the favourable economic situation and the work-sharing arrangement as well as the other concessions of the management, was accepted by the works councils including the one from Emden. At this point, the way to a unanimous decision on the supervisory board was open.[6]

The supervisory board decision
When the supervisory board met on 23 April to consider the US plant project, not a single aspect of the complex agreement negotiated between the union and the management had been formalised. The

procedure was that the understandings reached during the negotiations were to be included in the management's presentation to the supervisory board and into the minutes of the meeting. After the board had heard the management's report it approved the US project by unanimous vote.

In substantive terms, the decision provided for an assembly plant with up to 5,500 workers and a capacity of 800 cars per day (200,000 a year). The plant was to go into operation in the second half of 1977 with a workforce of 2,000. Two and a half years later, it was expected to reach full capacity. The size of the investment until the start of production was estimated at about DM 400–500 million. Engines, gear boxes and other labour-intensive parts would continue to be built in Germany while the remaining parts – equivalent to about two-thirds of total production costs – would be bought in the United States from American suppliers. The plant was to assemble only one model, the American version of the Golf (the 'Rabbit'). It was estimated that the plant would become profitable in about 1982/83.

As to the assurances given to the workers' representatives, one was that the American-built cars would not be sold in Europe. In this respect, the union and the works council were particularly sensitive, as shortly before the supervisory board meeting Brazilian-built Volkswagens had surfaced in Portugal. To reassure the union, Schmücker wrote a letter to Loderer stating that cars assembled in the US plant would not be sold outside North America. The letter was formally inserted into the records of the supervisory board.

Secondly, the management presented the board with a 'utilisation scheme' (*Belegungsplan*) for the domestic plants which covered the period until 1985 and which ensured that Emden stayed in operation with a workforce of about 6,000. In the long run, Emden was to produce the American version of the Audi 80 ('Fox') and parts of the Passat. In its presentation to the supervisory board, the management announced that between DM 30–40 million had been set aside for investment in Emden. Among other things, it was intended to build a new factory. Apart from whatever economic reasons there may have been for this, the decision indicated the continuing commitment of the company to its Emden plant and in this sense was of great psychological significance. Other elements of the utilisation scheme described in great detail the future distribution of work between the other German plants.[7]

Finally, and perhaps most importantly, the management gave to the supervisory board an assessment of the development of domestic employment in the German plants 'well into the 1980s'. The presentation came to the conclusion that 'the production of the Golf in the United States will have no adverse effect on employment in the German plants. On the contrary, it will rather contribute to making domestic employment at Volkswagen more secure' (Volkswagen press release, April 23). The statement was included in the minutes of the supervisory board. It represented the compromise reached between the two sides in their negotiations on the question of an 'employment guarantee'. Its precise meaning from the position of the management was explained by Schmücker in a television interview shortly after the supervisory board meeting had ended:

> *Schmücker:* In relation to our decision to produce the Rabbit in the United States, we have expressed the view that our middle and long run sales forecasts indicate that the feared effect on employment will not take place. We have stated that the number of workers we have at present will remain constant unless the heavens fall.
> *Reporter:* Is this a declaration of intent or a binding commitment? If sales were to go down again, this would have to have consequences, would it not?
> *Schmücker:* Everybody has understood that should economic conditions deteriorate, this intention, which we have stated very seriously, would have to be seen in a different light.

The corresponding statements by the workers representatives differed by a significant nuance. Also shortly after the supervisory board meeting, Loderer was interviewed by a radio reporter.

> *Reporter:* . . . It is apparent that the guarantee of employment you have asked for was not given. Does this mean that the IGM had to give way?
> *Loderer:* I am of a different opinion . . . Provided that nothing completely unpredictable happens – like another oil crisis – we can proceed on the assumption that the management has given the assurance to go as far as possible to protect employment, and only after this assurance had been given was unanimity possible . . .

An IGM press release of the same day went even further in maintaining that the management board had 'given the employment guarantees asked for by the workers' representatives'. Likewise, in a pamphlet distributed in the week after the decision in the German Volkswagen plants, the union described the events as follows:

> The management presented forecasts asserting that the US assembly plant would not destroy jobs in Germany. But it is a long way from mere assertions to reliable guarantees. The representatives of the workers made it unmistakeably clear that without such guarantees they would not agree. In response, the planning was considerably specified until guesses became certainties, and rough estimates became concrete predictions. Last Friday the project was finally ready to be decided upon.

It is small wonder, then, that the public debate after the decision both inside and outside the union centred largely on the credibility and the legal status of the management's assurances on employment. Whereas the IGM leadership tried to make the 'employment guarantee' appear as binding and formal as possible, the left-wing opposition in the union, and the executive committee of the Communist Party, spoke of a 'big hoax' and a 'pseudo agreement' which did not force the management into anything. In a technical sense, of course, this was certainly true; even the IGM leadership never claimed that the 'employment guarantee' was enforceable in court. On the other hand, since union and works council shared the management's optimistic assumptions on the company's economic prospects, from their perspective this problem was merely academic. While the agreement did indeed leave the management a way out in case it felt that it needed one,[8] the union was sure that such a need would not arise. One reason for its optimism was that by holding on to the new, conservative employment policy, the union itself could contribute to making the realisation of the 'employment guarantee' possible. The interpretation by the union of a trend forecast as a political agreement implied, in this sense, an acceptance of responsibility for making the forecast come true and, in particular, for keeping the workforce small enough to make reductions unnecessary.[9]

Because of the preoccupation of the public with the question of whether the 'employment guarantee' was binding or not, other aspects of the supervisory board decision which were of greater practical significance were overlooked. The presentation by the management to the supervisory board had been unusually specific and had contained commitments to future decisions which are normally under the sole jurisdiction of the management board. Since the entire presentation had been recorded in the minutes, it had become, in the view of the IGM, part and parcel of the supervisory board decision. In this sense, the 23 April meeting had set a precedent for an extension of the jurisdiction of the supervisory board in relation to the management board. Since supervisory boards are subject to union influence through co-determination, German unions have for a long time demanded that the powers of supervisory boards *vis-à-vis* the management be strengthened. In the present case, this demand was formally complied with through a passage in the supervisory board resolution saying that, 'The supervisory board, in accordance with the presentation of the management board, proceeds on the assumption that major changes of the concept presented today require its assent'. Two weeks later, the *Handelsblatt* – a journal representing the viewpoint of the business community – criticised Schmücker for having admitted the creation of 'a precedent for the future practice of co-determination'. Quoting IGM sources, the journal argued that in at least three areas, any major changes of elements of the US plant decision would now require the formal agreement of the supervisory board: changes in the extent to which the US plant used German-produced parts; changes in the plant utilisation scheme provided that they were related to the US investment; and changes concerning the re-importation ban. The *Handelsblatt* commented: 'This will be the practice of the new kind of co-determination. The supervisory boards will bring the most important management decisions under their jurisdiction, or they will bind the management by specific instructions and guarantees'. Later, the IGM frequently pointed to this article as confirmation of its view of the legal implications of the supervisory board decision.

On the other hand, while the legal aspects of the 23 April decision were undoubtedly important, what counted even more in practical terms was that during the process the confidence of both sides in the other's readiness to co-operate in good faith had been confirmed and reinforced. At the time of the final decision, this confidence had grown so strong that the diverging public interpretations of the 'employment guarantee' could be tolerated by both union and management. For the union, the most important thing was that the management had committed itself to do its utmost to prevent any adverse employment effects from the US project. For the management, on the other hand, the crucial point was that if there were to be, against all probabilities, another crisis, it would not be nailed down on an 'employment guarantee' given under different economic conditions, but could expect a 'reasonable, economically rational, co-operative' attitude.

It is important to understand that the readiness of a trade union to co-operate with management presupposes a sense of power. The power of a union can be defined in terms of the indispensability of its co-operation for the manageability of the firm. The more the management needs the union to perform its own function, the higher a price it is prepared to pay for co-operation. Conversely, the more the union knows that the management is dependent on it, the less afraid it will be of being taken advantage of in a co-operative relationship.

The price strong unions can get for their co-operation can be of an institutional or of an economic kind; often, it is both. In institutional terms, union co-operation requires from the management a sharing of managerial prerogatives; at Volkswagen, this took the form of a partly informal and partly formalised extension of co-determination. Economically, co-operation may have to be paid for by less-than-optimal solutions to economic problems when the optimal solution would violate vital union interests. In the case of S1, the price paid was that a plant was kept in operation which, from a purely economic point of view, should have been shut down. In the case of the US project, it was the reduction of the US plant to an assembly plant which was clearly suboptimal in economic terms but inevitable for political reasons. This was openly admitted by Schmücker. In his television interview on 23 April, Schmücker was asked whether 'the decision to transfer production to the United States only in stages was not more expensive? In other words, have you not paid tribute to the arguments of the union and the works council?' To this Schmücker replied:

> 'It is beyond doubt that it would of course have been less expensive to produce everything in the United States. This is, however, not a matter of paying a tribute to the union but rather one of the common insight that with the gradual approach two things can be realised. First, we reduce our financial commitment and with it our risk. And secondly, we minimise the risk to employment which in the last weeks and months has understandably been very much on the minds of our workers.'

The same subject was taken up even more explicitly in a background article in the conservative daily *Deutsche Zeitung*:

> It was clear to the supervisory board members, among them the top bankers Poullain (Westdeutsche Landesbank), Christians (Deutsche Bank) and Hesselbach (Bank für Gemeinwirtschaft), that they were agreeing to the more costly solution. It would have been cheaper if employment in the German plants had been cut back. However, discussion of such an 'unsocial' alternative was out of the question in view of unemployment being above one million. Nobody is to lose their job because of the transfer of production to the United States.

Outlook

One essential characteristic of the April 1976 supervisory board decision was that it allowed for considerable flexibility in the case of unexpected changes of the economic situation. In a sense, it could be said that the substance of the decision was less important than the procedure laid down in it, or implied by it for future amendments. The reason why the IGM had been able to agree to such flexibility in substance was that it was granted in exchange additional 'procedural' rights to co-determination. What difference these would have made if the development on the European car market had failed to meet the optimistic assumptions held by both sides at the time of the decision is unknown; until mid-1980, the new Volkswagen boom was unbroken, and the 'employment guarantee' could therefore be kept in full. Another element of the 1976 package that did not come up for reconsideration was the ban on re-importation which, as the management was well aware, is in normal circumstances not negotiable by the union.

A different case was what had been agreed in relation to the 'depth of production' in the American plant. The reason why this was inevitably to reappear on the agenda was the continuing decline of the dollar. The more the value of the dollar declined against the mark in the second half of the 1970s, the greater became the economic pressure on the company to transfer a higher proportion of production to the US than had originally been planned. In principle, this did not come as a surprise to the union. From the beginning, it had been more or less clear to the

IGM leadership that one day in the future the assembly plant would turn into a full-fledged production plant. The decision of April 1976, however it was formulated at the time, was clearly understood to be a first step in this direction. The reason why the US project had been acceptable to the union in spite of this was that, unlike under the old Leiding plans, the transfer of production to the United States was to be spread over a long period of time and was to take place with the close and continuous involvement of the union. For the IGM, this difference more than justified the considerable efforts made to change the management's original project.

It is interesting to note that the institutional set-up of the US plant is designed in such a way as to make an expansion of the scope of production relatively easy. Legally, Volkswagen of America is an independent company under United States law with its own board of directors. Demands of members of the Volkswagen central works council at a certain stage of the negotiations for a representative of the central works council to sit on the board of the American subsidiary were not accepted – not even, it appears, by the IGM leadership. Among the reasons given for this were language problems and doubts as to the legal feasibility. More important, however, seems to have been the desire to keep the option of a steady increase of the 'depth of production' in America as open as possible. If the central works council were represented on the American board of directors, the inevitable tendency of the German workplace representatives would be to resist an increase in production. Neither the management nor, it can be assumed, the union were prepared to concede this. The exclusion of the works council from the American board of directors means that the influence of the works council remains limited to the German negotiating system which is controlled on the labour side by the headquarters of the IGM. In these circumstances, it is to be expected that future decisions by the representatives of the Volkswagen workforce on the US plant will follow the same principles as the decision of 23 April, 1976.[10]

Footnotes
[1] Not counting the small assembly plant in Brussels.
[2] When in 1975 and 1976 the IGM was criticised in public for having prevented a timely decision in favour of a plant in the United States the then managing director, Schmücker, confirmed several times in press interviews that a decision on this subject had never been on the supervisory board's agenda. These statements contributed considerably to the good relationship between union and management.
[3] In another press interview on 15 April, Loderer said that talks were under way between union and management to determine the causes of Volkswagen's productivity gap.

4 On 9 March 1976 Loderer stated in a press interview that he agreed with the cautious approach to new employment at Volkswagen: 'Instead of expanding the workforce too early one should, with a view to the US project, try instead to satisfy the excess demand as far as possible through overtime.'

5 The internal consensus on the side of the workers representatives was summarised by Loderer in a press interview on 6 March. Loderer said the US project could be supported 'only if no workman in Germany loses his job as a consequence.'

6 The kind of solution that was envisaged was outlined very precisely by Loderer in a press interview on 15 April, a week before the supervisory board meeting. Loderer, according to the report, was 'confident that Volkswagen's managing director, Schmücker, would give *the requested information* since he knows that everything depends on this. "Our problems are also Herr Schmücker's problems." The IGM chief openly declared his sympathy with the former Rheinstahl boss. "Unlike Herr Leiding, who in his contacts with the workers' representatives had not always been co-operative, Schmücker is a man who likes *information* and *gives information*." (Author's italics.)

7 The implementation of the plant utilisation scheme caused considerable inconvenience to the workers and threw up manifold problems which had to be regulated by a large number of works agreements. In late 1977, the redistribution of work among the German plants was still in progress. At a works meeting in Braunschweig, the chairman of the central works council, Ehlers, had to defend the relocation of production against heavy criticism. Ehlers argued that it was necessary to save jobs. Following the presentation by the management to the central works council of a detailed updated utilisation scheme in September 1977, works agreements had to be negotiated on matters such as the number of engines of a certain type to be produced during the following five years in a certain plant; the gradual transfer of production of the rear axle of a certain model from one plant to another; the transfer of workers within plants to new jobs without loss of pay and seniority and so on. The kind of problems confronting the works councils as a consequence of the US plant compromise can be seen from a leaflet distributed by the Wolfsburg works council in late 1977 which defended the transfer of a particular part away from the Braunschweig plant by pointing out that 'our Braunschweig colleagues urgently need work.' The works council went on to emphasise that 'we have agreed to the transfer only after a binding commitment had been made by the management that those affected will get equivalent jobs in the same wage grade. The reorganisation will take place step by step until 1979. This will make a smooth transfer of workers to new jobs possible.'

8 The IGM was expressly commended for this by the conservative *Deutsche Zeitung*: 'The fact that IGM chairman, Loderer, and the other IGM supervisory board members were not demanding a job guarantee but only a declaration of intent speaks in favour of Loderer's economic reason. In other words, if the business cycle acts against them, Volkswagen workers in the Federal Republic will lose their jobs and assembly in the United States will nevertheless be expanded.'

9 In addition, interview material shows that the IGM hoped for an increase of overall sales as a result of production in the United States. In this case, only part of the output of the US plant would have been at the expense of

German production and German employment. The IGM leadership and their advisers were aware that acting on this premise involved a considerable risk; as one interviewee put it: 'one can only hope that it will come true'.

[10] In 1980, the Volkswagen plant in Westmoreland, USA, had reached its final capacity of 1,000 cars a day on schedule. On 11 April, the supervisory board agreed unanimously to a proposal by the management to set up a second assembly plant in the United States. The plant, which is to be located near Detroit, is to start production in the second half of 1982; its capacity is planned to be 800 cars a day.

7 The Politics of Overtime

The demand for motor cars is subject to strong fluctuations. Every year, sales tend to rise in the spring and decline in the winter. More importantly, the market is highly sensitive to the general business cycle. If prospective car buyers are uncertain about their future income, the purchase of a new car is likely to be postponed. This applies in particular to replacement purchases. Since with growing car ownership in industrialised countries the proportion of replacement purchases in the car market is increasing, cyclical fluctuations are likely to become more accentuated in the future.

Changes in demand for cars translate relatively directly into changes in the industry's demand for labour. The main reason for this is that cars are difficult and, in any case, expensive to store. Thus, in periods of declining demand producers have only limited capacity to build up stocks. Correspondingly, when the market picks up, existing stocks tend to be too small to satisfy the additional demand. As a result, car producers have to respond to changes in the market directly by adjusting their production and, thus, their input of labour.

In the car industry just as in other industries, managements have two ways of adjusting their labour input: they can change the size of their labour force, or they can change the amount of input obtained from the existing labour force. The first alternative includes the employment of new workers and/or the dismissal of old ones. The second alternative is for the existing workforce either to work more (overtime) or to work less (short-time) than usual. The two approaches can be combined in that a company may call overtime while simultaneously taking on new workers, or work short-time while also dismissing workers. Furthermore, a company may use overtime or employ new workers in one department, or category of employment, while at the same time calling short-time work or dismissing workers in others.

In all western countries, the car industry has in the past been a classical example of a 'hire-and-fire' industry. In addition to the impact of the industry's strong business fluctuations and its limited possibilities for stocking its products, a large proportion of the workforce is unskilled, and no long training is required for new entrants. This tends to make labour turnover inexpensive. As a result, strong cyclical changes in the size of the workforce, following and replicating the changes in the industry's business cycle, have for long been the normal condition in the industry.

Workforce	Product Demand	
	Rising	Falling
Kept constant	Overtime	Short-time work
Changed	Additional employment	Dismissals

Employment stability, short-time work, and overtime: A trade union perspective

One of the foremost objectives of trade unions representing car workers has always been to protect their members' employment and income from the fluctuations in the business cycle as far as possible. Unions in the car industry have traditionally pressed for institutional provisions of one kind or another by which the sensitivity of the industry's labour input to the changes in the demand for its products is reduced. The two goals that can be distinguished in this respect are *employment security* and *income security*. Employment security can be achieved, and the practice of 'hiring and firing' abolished, either through legal regulations preventing employers from dismissing workers and/or by making dismissals, by whatever means, more expensive. One side effect of dismissals becoming more difficult or more costly is, of course, that employers become more reluctant to take on new workers. While this is certainly not what unions aim at, it is not unacceptable for those who are already employed and whose employment security is increased.

Workers in secure employment have an interest in protecting their income from being temporarily reduced as a result of shortage of work. Temporary lay-offs resulting in a loss of pay are referred to in the present discussion as 'short-time work'. (In some countries, including Germany, the social security system under certain conditions makes up for part of the wages lost by workers in a period of short-time work; see p. 108). Unions may try to prevent employers from laying off workers temporarily by placing material disincentives on a discontinuous allocation of work over time. To the extent that they are successful in this, they may cause a reduction not only of short-time work in periods of market decline but also of overtime in times of peak demand. Overtime, however, is usually better paid than normal working time, and its reduction in favour of a continuous allocation of work may be a negative side-effect of increased income security.[1]

Employment security and income security may be in partial conflict with each other. The more successful unions are in preventing dismissals, the more employers – everything else being equal – will have to rely on short-time work in periods of market decline. Furthermore, the more employers are forced by strong employment protection to be conservative in taking on additional workers, the more they will tend to rely on overtime in times of rising demand. In other words, security of employment is relatively easy to obtain if workers are prepared to make sacrifices of income security, and the income of employed workers is easier to stabilise if the size of the workforce is permitted to fluctuate.

To understand the strategic problems of trade unions trying to stabilise their members' employment and income, further qualifications have to be introduced three of which should specifically be mentioned. First, unions may be prepared to agree to some 'hiring and firing' among marginal groups of the workforce – for example, unskilled foreign workers – in order to protect the employment of their core membership. Generally speaking, any group of workers may be tempted to accept other groups being dismissed (or laid off) if this increases their own security. Whether or not a given group will be able to impose the costs of its security on other groups depends to a great deal on the structure of the union organisation and the industrial relations system.

Secondly, overtime as a way of meeting increased product demand is not only acceptable but welcome to workers provided that it does not exceed a certain limit, that it is well paid, and that it does not pave the way for future short-time work. Overtime is the better paid the more expensive it is for the employer to dismiss newly employed workers. By increasing employment security, unions thus not only increase the incentives for employers to use overtime instead of new employment, but also make it attractive for the existing – and probably undersized – workforce to work overtime.

Thirdly, short-time work may also be acceptable to workers provided that the losses of income associated with it are small. In Germany in the late 1970s, State-financed short-time work benefits amounted to about 85 per cent of a worker's take-home pay. Normally, workers on short-time work are laid off for about a quarter of their monthly working hours. When a German car factory works short-time, workers stay home for one week a month; for this time, they get short-time work benefits from the State. Over the entire month, this results in a loss of income of about four per cent. With two weeks of short-time work – which is an extreme and very rare case – monthly income losses amount to about eight per cent.

A works council asked by the management to agree to one or two weeks of short-time usually is under strong pressure from the workforce to acquiesce. Workers especially in rural areas welcome a short lay-off as an opportunity to tend to their gardens, repair their houses, help relatives with the tillage, and so on. Moreover, many workers go moonlighting during lay-off periods, and together with the short-time work benefits, they can earn much more than in normal weeks. The situation becomes different, however, when short-time work continues for several consecutive months. With time, income losses accumulate and fear of dismissals will become more and more widespread. After several months of short-time work, workers will urge the works council to press for restoration of normal working hours. Unions and works councils have to reflect this tendency in their policies.

Organisation of overtime in the car industry

Overtime and short-time work affect different groups of workers differently depending on their position in the organisation of work. Since most white-collar workers rarely work short-time or overtime, they are disregarded in the following. Among blue-collar workers, the situation differs between assembly line workers (in Germany called productive or direct workers) and maintenance workers or toolmakers (non-productive or indirect workers).[2] Changes in product demand have immediate effects on the 'productive workers' only. The demand for 'non-productive' or 'indirect' workers is, in the short and medium term, independent of the number of cars produced. It is possible, and in fact not infrequent, that indirect workers have to work overtime while direct workers are on short-time work or are even being dismissed. The most common example is in periods of model change when the toolmakers have to work in three shifts around the clock while demand for the old models declines and stocks have to be cleared. Because of its specific connection to product demand and employment security overtime for direct workers figures much more prominently in workplace industrial relations and collective bargaining than overtime for indirect workers, and it is almost exclusively with the former that the present case study will be concerned.

Production workers in German car factories work overtime in the form of eight-hour overtime shifts at the weekend (*Sonderschichten*) rather than single hours added to a work-day. This is because of the general organisation of working hours in the German car industry. Car factories in Germany work in two shifts of eight hours each from Monday to Friday. There is no interruption of production between the first and second shift. The first shift normally works from 6.00 to 14.00 hours, and the second shift starts at 14.00 and ends at 22.00 hours. After the second shift, maintenance workers come in for urgent or complicated repairs. Since in these circumstances neither of the two production shifts can be extended beyond eight hours, the only possible way of working overtime is through additional shifts which are usually scheduled for Saturday mornings. The normal procedure is that those workers who have worked the first shift during the week come in also on Saturday from 6.00 to 14.00 hours. In the following week when the other half of the productive workforce is working the first shift, these come in on the Saturday morning to work their overtime shift. Each worker can thus work a maximum of eight hours overtime every two weeks. (It is also possible, of course, that two shifts are worked on Saturday so that workers get eight hours of overtime per week; but this almost never happens.) Given a normal 40-hour working week, overtime can increase a production worker's working time by at most ten per cent (16 hours per month added to 160 regular hours). Overtime shifts are always scheduled in even numbers (either two or four or six and so on) to distribute the work and the extra pay, evenly over the two halves of the productive workforce. Other ways of organising overtime are of course conceivable – for example, working four instead of eight hours on Saturdays – but since any arrangement requires the approval of the works council (see p. 111), managerial discretion on this matter is narrowly limited in practice.[3]

Up to ten per cent of the workers for whom an overtime shift has been scheduled may choose to stay home. If more than this proportion of the shift apply for (unpaid) leave, the foreman and the works council decide jointly who has to come to work. (Works councils normally base such decisions on a number of general criteria like age, sex, and family status so that married women with children or older workers are more likely to be given leave than young unmarried men). However, it is very infrequent that the ten per cent limit is reached. Normally, the proportion of workers who are prepared to work overtime far exceeds 90 per cent. While managers explain this by the high pay workers get for overtime, works councillors suggest that it also is to do with a need to make up for past or future short-time work. They also say that workers fear to appear unreliable by not showing up, as this might make them candidates for dismissal in the case of a reduction of the workforce.

In May 1977, an average production worker at Opel in Rüsselsheim earned DM 11.65 per hour and DM 93.20 for an eight hours working day. For an overtime shift, he got a bonus of DM 15 for his attendance, and his pay for the eight hours exceeded his normal pay by about 46 per cent. Together with the bonus, this amounted to a total pay increase of about 62 per cent (to DM 151.10). With one overtime shift per month, an average worker's monthly pay thus rose by about eight per cent; with two overtime shifts, the increase amounted to about 16 per cent.[4]

Manpower policy and co-determination

Trade unions in West Germany exercise their influence on a company's manpower policy mainly through the works council. Works councils have legal rights to participate in decisions affecting the utilisation of labour, in particular – but by no means exclusively – in decisions on the size of the labour force and the use of overtime or short-time work. On the latter two subjects, the Works Constitution Act of 1972 stipulates in Section 87,1,3 that the works council 'shall have a right of co-determination on . . . any temporary reduction or extension of the hours normally worked in the establishment'. Co-determination, here as throughout the Works Constitution Act, means that the employer must have the assent of the works council before he can take action. If employer and works council do not reach an agreement, the matter can be put by either side before a conciliation committee. According to Section 87,2 'the award of the Conciliation Committee (takes) the place of an agreement' between the two parties.

The composition and the functions of conciliation committees are determined by Section 76 of the Act. Conciliation committees consist 'of assessors appointed in equal number by the employer and the works council, and of an independent chairman accepted by both sides'. If no agreement on a chairman can be reached, he or she is appointed by the Labour Court. The conciliation committee decides by majority vote. However, in the first round of voting after the oral proceedings have been concluded, the chairman is supposed not to cast his vote but to wait for a majority to form among the party representatives. If the first vote results in a tie, 'the discussion shall be resumed and the chairman shall participate in the subsequent vote' (Section 76,3). Either of the parties can appeal to the Labour Court against an award by a conciliation committee 'on the grounds that the conciliation committee has exceeded its powers'. Conciliation committees are provided for in many places in the Works Constitution Act as a mechanism for breaking deadlocks over matters under co-determination.

The legal situation concerning short-time work is special since in this case the Works Constitution Act is partly superseded by the *Arbeitsförderungsgesetz* (Employment Promotion Act). If an employer can show to the labour administration that without a temporary lay-off he would have to dismiss workers, the administration may officially grant the lay-off and pay the affected workers short-time work benefits from unemployment insurance funds. Under the Employment Promotion Act, the labour administration has to 'hear' the works council before it decides. Employers intending to apply for short-time work therefore usually try to enlist the support of their works council although short-time work can be granted without the works council's consent. In this case, the right to co-determination under Section 87,1,3 extends only to the way in which short-time work is instituted.

Co-determination rights on the employment of new workers are even stronger than on overtime. Section 99,1 of the Works Constitution Act determines that the employer has to 'notify the works council in advance of any engagement' of new employees. Employers have to submit to the works council 'the appropriate recruitment documents and . . . information on the persons concerned'. Furthermore, they have to 'inform the works council of the implications of the action envisaged, supply it with the necessary supporting documentation and obtain its consent to the action envisaged'. Section 99,2 stipulates that the works council 'may refuse its consent' if, among other things, 'there is factual reason to assume that the action is likely to result in dismissals or will in some other way prejudice the rights of the employees of the establishment not warranted by operational or personal reasons'. If the works council does not agree with the employer on a matter covered by Section 99, the employer cannot call upon the conciliation committee but has to go directly to the Labour Court.

Co-determination rights are weakest with regard to dismissals. Under Section 102,1 of the Act, works councils have to be 'consulted before every dismissal' and given the reasons for the dismissals. If the works council has not been consulted, a dismissal is 'null and void'. Works councils may formally oppose dismissals on a number of grounds. The most important of these (Section 102,3,1) is that the employer 'in selecting the employee to be dismissed disregarded or did not take sufficient account of social considerations'.[5] If the works council objects to a dismissal, the employer may proceed with it but can be taken by the works council to the Labour Court. Apart from this, the employer can be sued by the dismissed workers for violation of individual employment rights under the Employment Protection Act. (Here, the employee is normally represented by his or her union.)

The most important category of dismissals for the present study is dismissals for economic reasons. In this respect, the German law leaves employers considerable discretion. If an employer observes the procedural rules laid down in the Works Constitution Act and the individual rights of employees under the Employment Protection Act, he can dismiss up to 49 workers a month. If he wants to dismiss more, he has to apply to the labour administation for a *Massenentlassung* (mass dismissal). A *Massenentlassung* must be permitted if the employer can show that it is necessary to protect the economic viability of the enterprise and the employment of the rest of the workforce. On this, the labour administration has to 'hear' the works council. An employer whose application for a *Massenentlassung* has been granted has to negotiate with the works council on a 'social plan'. If no agreement can be reached, a conciliation committee is set up which can make a binding award. The co-determination rights of the works council under Section 102,3 remain in effect, and so do the employment protection rights of individual employees. (Section 102 does not, however, apply to severance payments schemes; they are not formally subject to co-determination.)

The legal rights of works councils in relation to overtime, short-time work, new employment and dismissals carry with them difficult obligations and critical and unpleasant choices. For example, employers in order to avoid being found in violation of Section 102,3,1 may ask their works council for a works agreement specifying the 'social considerations' to be observed in dismissals. Frequently, employers go as far as to ask the works council to advise them in selecting the individuals to be dismissed. Likewise, owing to their strong legal position, works councils in periods of economic decline have to make a choice between short-time work and dismissals, and in periods of expansion they have to choose between additional employment and overtime. Both choices are equally difficult. In the latter case the works council has to strike a balance between the interests of unemployed workers who would like to have a job and the interest of employed workers who would like to increase their income through overtime. The risk of leaning too much towards the first interest is that these workers may become involved in mass dismissals later when the boom has ended. The risk associated with representing the second interest is that overtime, if called too frequently, may become unpopular. Which alternative a works council adopts is not independent of how it expects the market to develop. If the upswing is strong and lasting, a works council can afford to press for additional employment and may, nevertheless, be able to get a limited amount of overtime for the existing workforce. However, if the upswing is weak and shortlived, it is rational for a works council to opt exclusively for overtime. Since the risks associated with an expanded workforce are undoubtedly severer than the risks associated with overtime, it is politically safer for works councils to work on conservative assumptions and to prefer, whenever possible, overtime to new employment.

The place of overtime in workplace industrial relations

The co-determination rights of works councils on overtime are important for the general conduct of workplace industrial relations. Works councils may use co-determination rights to extend their influence to subjects that formally are beyond their jurisdiction. One of these subjects is pay bargaining. By threatening not to co-operate on matters subject to co-determination, works councils of firms with above-average economic performance may get their employers to bargain with them over wages and to agree to pay increases which are additional to the industrial agreement. Among the co-determination rights that are most frequently used for this purpose is that on overtime. Works councils asked by their employers to agree to overtime usually respond by asking for something in return. Shift bonuses, higher overtime rates and other items closely related to overtime are only one category of the compensations demanded by works councils in exchange for overtime. Other demands include additional holidays, additional breaks, changes in piece rates, Christmas bonuses, profit sharing arrangements, changes in the wage grade structure reducing the wage differentials between the lowest and the highest grade, and general wage increases in the 'second wage round'. A specialty of the car industry is agreements giving workers an option to buy cars produced during an overtime shift at a 15–20 per cent discount. Employers faced with demands of this kind may feel that the works council abuses its legal powers, and they may even be sure that their position would be upheld in court. But asking for a conciliation committee or going to the Labour Court is not a solution since it is too time-consuming. Overtime typically is needed urgently and when at the end of a lengthy legal procedure the objections of the works council are finally overridden, the employer may then no longer need the workforce to work overtime. It is this dependence of the employer on a speedy positive decision which makes the right to co-determination on overtime one of the works council's most effective bargaining devices.

The following two accounts examine the policies on overtime of the works councils of two major German car producers, Volkswagen and Opel Rüsselsheim, during the car boom in the mid to late 1970s. The cases reflect a situation which was new to both works councillors and personnel managers in at least two important respects: the Works Constitution Act of 1972 had just come into operation, and for the first time in the history of the Federal Republic there was high and continuing unemployment. Both case studies describe attempts by works councils to use their co-determination rights on overtime to influence their employer's general manpower policy. While in the first case the foremost goal of the works council was steady employment, in the second it was, at least periodically, a reduction of unemployment. Although the attitudes and ideologies of the two works councils differed strongly – resulting in intense factional conflict within the union – the actual effects of their policies turned out to be surprisingly similar. In this respect, the two cases demonstrate the importance of the institutional framework as a determinant of the substantive outcomes of industrial relations.

The experience at Volkswagen

One of the lasting consequences of the 1974 crisis at Volkswagen was that both management and works council changed their attitudes on employment policy. By the end of August 1975, a few months after sales had begun to pick up again, all stocks were cleared and demand continued to rise. While in the Leiding era the management would at this point probably have employed new workers, it now asked the works councils at Wolfsburg and Emden for no less than 14 overtime shifts to be distributed over the remaining 17 weeks of the year. (For the individual production worker in each of the two plants, this meant that he or she would have to report to work on seven Saturdays during the coming four months.) The request was immediately granted, and apparently no effort was made by the works councils to get more than the usual overtime bonus in return.

By mid-October, it had become clear that the boom was so strong that overtime alone was not sufficient. As a first step, the management lifted the recruitment ban for production workers in Wolfsburg as far as necessary to compensate for wastage. Two weeks later, the recruitment ban for Emden was lifted, and agreement was reached with the works council to take on 5,000 new workers at Wolfsburg in the first six months of 1976. Over half of these (2,700) were expected to replace wastage while the rest would add to the size of the workforce. Works council and central works council gave their consent only after the management had undertaken not to dismiss any worker during 1976. Furthermore, the management had to agree not to ask for short-time work within a period of three months after the last overtime shift, so that there would be an interval of at least a quarter year between overtime and short-time work. In the other plants, the recruitment ban remained in force as a measure to improve productivity.

That the agreement provided for relatively few new workers had implications for both the works council and the management. With demand continuing to rise, the implication for the works council was that it would have to agree to more overtime shifts in the future. For the management, the agreement implied that it would employ no more additional workers than could be kept on in the event of a new crisis, and that it could ask for overtime only if it was sure that short-time work would not be necessary within three months. In effect, this meant that the company would sell fewer cars during the year than it could have done, given the still-rising demand.

At some point in 1976, works council and management began to refer to their new approach to employment as *Beschäftigungspolitik der mittleren Linie* (middle-line employment policy). The new policy reflected both the exigencies created by the US plant project and the experience of the S1 redundancy programme. During the whole of 1976, the works council responded favourably to requests for overtime but asked for higher employment and income security for the existing workforce in return. Thus, the obligation of the management to observe a time interval between overtime and short-time work was continually renewed, and so was the ban on dismissals for a period of six months running from the time of the last overtime shift. Furthermore, the management agreed to one paid holiday between Christmas and New

Year and higher overtime pay. The works council, in exchange, refrained from pressing for additional employment.

How the new policy was presented to the workforce can be seen from an article in the central works council's newsletter of March 1977. The article, signed by the chairman of the central works council, Ehlers, carried the headline, *New Employment Policy A Success*. It reminded its readers of 'the infamous S1 scheme' and continued:

> This must not happen again! After this painful experience and as a result of lengthy negotiations we have reached an agreement with the management on a *Beschäftigungspolitik der mittleren Linie*. This new policy is designed to permit smooth adjustment to business fluctuations by combining additional employment and overtime work. By now we can conclude that this employment policy was successful. The number of 3,000 new workers that was originally agreed upon has been far exceeded. On the other hand, only as many new workers have been taken on as Volkswagen can employ over a longer period of time. It makes no sense to employ thousands of workers only to dismiss them a short time later. The age of 'hire and fire' must be over at Volkswagen.

However, not everybody was as happy as the works council with the new policy. The mere fact that this article had to appear at all, and the way in which it was written, indicates that in early 1977, the support of the workforce for the cautious approach taken by the works council was dwindling. Throughout 1976, most production workers had been working every second Saturday. While this had certainly increased their income, now many felt tired and wanted to return to normal working hours. Moreover, in some plants the general recruitment ban was still in force, and with the workforce declining as a result of natural wastage, the intensity of work for those who remained behind had been continually increasing for almost two years. The works councils of these plants began to press with growing urgency for additional employment. The most important opportunity for the opposition to express itself was offered by works meetings attended by members of the national IGM leadership or the central works council. Beginning in the autumn of 1976, the union leadership and works councils were confronted with arguments like 'more work requires more workers' with increasing frequency. Since the Volkswagen boom had been going on for more than a year and promised to continue in the foreseeable future, it was argued that an increase in total employment was due.

The situation became critical in January 1977 when the central works council granted a request by the management for 12 more overtime shifts. The shifts were to be distributed over the first six months of the year so that production workers would be required to work overtime on one Saturday each month. This amounted to a reduction of overtime by one half. In a statement issued to the workforce, the central works council declared that from that time it would, as a matter of policy, permit no more than two overtime shifts per month (the level set by the January 1976 agreement). Apparently, however, this was not enough to overcome the resistance of the workforce. In addition, the works council had to persuade the management to give workers the option to buy the cars produced during some of the Saturday shifts at a 15 per cent discount.[6] The works council argued that because of the limited output – which was a consequence of the joint 'middle-line' employment policy – delivery terms for Volkswagen cars had become so long that many workers had not been able to buy new cars. It was only after the management had conceded this point that the works council felt it could agree to the 12 additional shifts.[7]

Even so, overtime remained controversial. Since the works council, because of the US plant project, felt it necessary not to increase employment too much, it had to go through some difficult political manoeuvering. By the end of April 1977, a note appeared in the central works council's newsletter announcing that 'overtime shifts will soon be over'. It ended with the consoling sentence: 'At our main competitors, Opel and Ford, workers also had to work a series of overtime shifts.'

The full meaning of this remark can be understood only against the background of the general labour market in West Germany at this time and of the ongoing debate on trade union policy especially within the IGM. During 1976 and 1977, the unemployment rate had been between four and five per cent of the workforce. One suggestion that had been put forward by politicians and trade unionists as a way of fighting unemployment was to restrict overtime in those sectors of the economy that were still booming. The most important of these was the car industry. The central works council of Volkswagen, having gone through the S1 experience and acting under the constraints of the US investment project, was, of course, less than enthusiastic about such proposals. From its perspective, it was not overtime that had to be restricted but rather recruitment, even if this might in the short run have the deplorable consequence of keeping unemployment high. While this position was supported by the IGM leadership it was not shared by the entire union. The left wing had by this time become increasingly vociferous in demanding a more 'solidaristic' approach to employment and urging the national executive to be less indulgent with the *Betriebsegoismus* of powerful works councils. For less idealistic reasons this position was shared by the works councils of the Volkswagen plants which were still subject to a total recruitment ban. Other pressures in the same direction came from the Federal Ministry of Labour. In this situation, it became increasingly difficult for the IGM leadership to stick to its policy.

The problems of the leadership were exacerbated by the fact that during 1976 and 1977, the works council of another important car factory, Opel at Rüsselsheim, pursued a policy of overtime that was, at least in its intentions, opposed to that of the Volkswagen works council. In a continuing confrontation with management which was given much publicity in the press, the Opel works council tried to prevent the company from using overtime as a substitute for the employment of new workers. While in reality the events were somewhat more complex, the politically important point was that they were perceived in this way by the public as well as by many union members and officials.

The tensions within the union came to a climax at an internal IGM car workers conference in Böblingen in January, 1977 – shortly after the Volkswagen central works council had agreed to the twelve overtime shifts for the first half of the year. In attendance at the conference – which met in private session – were the leading works council members of the car industry, the full time officials of union districts with car factories, the members of the national executive board, a number of headquarters officials concerned particularly with the car industry, and for the first time the *Vertrauensleute* leaders from the big car factories. All in all, there were about one hundred participants. One of the subjects discussed was overtime. Since the matter had long become entangled in the union's general pattern of factional conflict, the debate was heated and political. During the discussion, the (full time) chairman of the district of Emden took sides with the Opel works council against the central works council of Volkswagen. Loderer, who was present during the discussion, did not take the floor and made no attempt to settle the issue. However, he left no doubt that the 'middleline' policy of the Volkswagen central works council still had his support. To understand the implications of the events at Böblingen, it is necessary to take a closer look at the situation existing at this time at Opel Rüsselsheim.

The experience at Opel

There were mainly two reasons why the attitude of the works council at Rüsselsheim differed from that at Volkswagen: the specific experience with short-time work during the car crisis after 1973, and a change in the composition of the works council in favour of the left which coincided with the recovery of the car market in early 1975. When car sales began to decline in March 1973, Opel Rüsselsheim[8] had a workforce of about 38,000. Of these, about 15,000 were production workers, another 15,000 were skilled and maintenance workers, and the rest were white-collar workers. In February 1975 when the events analysed in this case study began, employment was down to 27,000, that is, by 27 per cent. Most of the losses were among production workers. There had been no forced redundancies, however, and the reduction of employment had been effected exclusively through natural wastage and severance payments.

One way by which forced redundancies had been avoided was extensive use of short-time work. In the 15 months between December 1973 and February 1975, workers had been laid off for 13 weeks, and they had grown increasingly impatient on short-time work especially since it was accompanied by a continuous decline of employment. Although the works council had agreed to short-time work only on condition that there would be no forced redundancies, workers had come to see the lay-offs as a sign of worse things to come. When the new car boom took off in the spring of 1975, these anxieties were still fresh in everyone's memory.

The second factor, the result of the works council election in May 1975, was related to the first. Both the union and the works council at Opel had a long history of factional strife. The crisis after 1973 had deepened the internal divisions to such an extent that the two factions had been unable to agree on a joint list of candidates. Tired of the perpetual political in-fighting and in order to have the matter settled one way or the other, IGM headquarters finally agreed to two separate IGM lists, one from the left and one from the right, competing for seats on the works council. The hope was that after the election had shown which side had stronger support among the electorate, the two wings would again join together under the leadership of the majority.

Among the central issues of the election campaign – which began shortly after the turn of the year – was manpower policy. The left, which on the existing works council was in the minority, accused the incumbent leadership of collusion with the management on short-time work. In an effort to capitalise on the growing resentment against short-time work, the opposition argued that the majority should have forced the management to plan its manpower use more carefully to make short-time work unnecessary. When in February 1975 the management once more suggested short-time work, it took the new political situation into account and proposed eight rather than ten days as previously. Under the pressure of the election campaign, the works council for the first time in years did not support the management's proposal in full and agreed to only six days. When the management dropped its request for short-time work rather than appeal to the labour administration, both factions of the works council were genuinely surprised.

Shortly after this event, car sales slowly began to pick up. In March 1975 the management for the first time in years asked for overtime in the press shop to speed up the ongoing model change. This sparked off a political controversy on the works council. Under its rules of procedure, requests for overtime for skilled workers in a single shop are handled by the works council member responsible for the particular shop. In the present case, this happened to be the leader and top candidate of the left faction, Richard Heller, who at this time was also the chairman of the *Vertrauensleute* body.

To be consistent with his election campaign, Heller would have had to deny the management's request. Given the position he had taken in his campaign statements, he should have objected to the abrupt change from short-time work to overtime and demanded that the management employ additional workers to fill the gaps caused by the severance payments scheme and the recruitment ban. On the other hand, most of the workers concerned were quite willing to work overtime to make up for the past losses of pay. In trying to protect his political fortunes, Heller decided to turn to the full works council arguing that the matter was of principal importance and that for a negative decision he needed the support of the works council as a whole. This support was refused, however, and the requested overtime was granted by majority vote. Shortly after this, with the meeting still under way, word came from the management that they were about to ask for six overtime shifts and the employment of five hundred additional production workers on fixed-term contracts. While Heller and his group stuck to their position and urged the works council to object, the vote went the same way, and the overtime shifts were granted.

While the works council was divided on the overtime issue, it was not on the fixed-term contracts. Normally, work contracts in Germany do not run out automatically so that workers enjoy full legal employment protection. Among blue-collar workers, fixed-term contracts are accepted mainly by foreign workers. The great majority of foreign workers, however, are on normal work contracts. Works councils generally do not permit fixed-term contracts because their holders are less protected than other workers. In the situation at Opel in early 1975, however,

Table 7.1   Results of Works Council Elections at Opel Rüsselsheim in May, 1975

List	Seats
IGM (Left)	20
IGM (Right)	13
Turkish workers	2
DAG	6
Christian metal workers	4
Total	45

even the left-wing minority felt that time limitation of the new contracts was acceptable given their low number and the extreme uncertainty of the economic situation.

The works council election of May 1975 resulted in a clear victory of the left IGM list over the right (Table 7.1). The left group led by Heller got 20 seats while the right group under the sitting works council chairman got no more than 13. The remaining 12 seats went to a list of Turkish workers supported by the IGM, to the DAG and to the Christian Metal Workers Association (whose relative electoral strength at Opel reflects the high proportion of Roman Catholics among the population in the Rüsselsheim area). A few days after the election, the works council elected Heller as its chairman with the votes of the two IGM lists and the Turkish list. His predecessor became chairman of the central works council formed by representatives of the works councils of Opel Rüsselsheim and Opel Bochum.[9]

First round: income maintenance during short-time work

A few days after the works council election, the management requested six more overtime shifts. In its response, the works council made its consent conditional on an assurance that no worker would be dismissed, transferred or down-graded for lack of work before the end of the year. In addition, it asked for an agreement under which the company would have had to pay workers on short-time work the difference between their short-time work compensation and their normal take-home pay.

Partly, the position of the works council reflected the political need for the new majority to exhibit a less co-operative attitude towards management than its predecessor. Moreover, the attitude of the works council was popular. The economic prospects for the summer and autumn appeared uncertain, and the income losses suffered during the protracted period of short-time work were not yet forgotten. If workers and works councillors agreed to work more overtime in the spring they might find that short-time work would be introduced again in the autumn. If the management argued, as it did, that a need for short-time work in the second half of the year could not be completely ruled out, then the company should at least guarantee that short-time work would no longer reduce workers' incomes.

There was still another, more general aspect to the works council's demands. With its response, the works council had created a link between overtime and short-time work. Using its co-determination rights on overtime as an instrument, the works council wanted to make short-time work more expensive for the company. The expectation was that with short-time work becoming more costly, the company would be less inclined to make use of it, and that it would have an incentive to even out the cyclical changes in its use of manpower. As a consequence, both overtime and short-time work would become less frequent. This theme was to be further developed and to figure even more prominently in the works council's policies during the following months and years.

Immediately after the management had been presented with the works council's response, it asked for conciliation. This was only the second time that a conciliation committee had been formed at Opel after the passage of the Works Constitution Act of 1972. (The first time was on a very minor issue – prices of meals at the cafeteria at Bochum.) Works councils and managements are generally reluctant to enter into conciliation. Once a committee has been set up, the respective issue is beyond the control of the two parties and no longer subject to their political give-and-take. Since both sides have an interest in preserving their ability to offer concessions to get other concessions in return, conciliation is used only as a last resort. When the Opel management in May 1975 asked for a conciliation committee, it meant to demonstrate that it considered the works council's demands unreasonable and non-negotiable. It also seems that it wanted to teach a new, inexperienced works council leadership a first and lasting lesson.

From the perspective of the works council, the risk of having an issue resolved through conciliation is that the chairman of the conciliation committee might not recognise the sublegal or illegal 'customs and practices' followed by the two parties in their direct dealings with one another. There is no clear legal definition of the kinds of compensation works councils may demand in return for a positive decision on a matter under co-determination. Nor is there consensus on whether a conciliation committee in making an award has to take into account the preceding informal negotiations between the parties. For example, a works council may refuse overtime because the management is not prepared to concede an additional holiday in exchange; instead, the management may offer an extra shift bonus of DM 20. If at this point the matter goes to conciliation, the chairman may decide to limit the proceedings to the question of whether or not it was reasonable for the works council to refuse the requested overtime – which is indeed the only issue officially before the committee. If the chairman then concludes that on the merits of the case, the management's request has to be granted, the works council not only has not won the additional holiday but also loses the extra shift bonus that had already been informally conceded.

In this particular instance the informal bargaining between the parties continued even though the conciliation committee had begun its work. Before the first vote was taken, a compromise was reached. The works council dropped its demand for an income guarantee for short-time workers. It had become clear during the proceedings that the chairman was not willing to go along with the works council on this point, so the decision was not difficult to make. The management, for its part, agreed not to dismiss workers during the remaining seven months of the year, and not to ask for short-time work during the five months until the end of October. It also agreed to change some of the fixed-term contracts awarded in March into normal work contracts. On these conditions, the works council agreed to the requested six overtime shifts.

The limited employment guarantee the new Opel works council had gained from management was regarded as a formidable breakthrough by IGM and by the general public. One year later when the Volkswagen works council negotiated a no-dismissals and no-short-time-work agreement in exchange for a number of overtime shifts (see p. 115) it was following the Rüsselsheim example. On the other hand, the new works council leadership knew that if the industry were again to decline, the agreement would not prevent short-time work and dismissals but would just postpone them. The goals of income maintenance during short-time work; of a more steady and less cyclical use of labour; and of replenishing the depleted work force had not become obsolete even though for the time being they had to recede into the background.

Second round: bargaining as usual
Early in 1975, the idea of reducing overtime as a way of raising employment did not play much of a role in the Opel works council's policy. Mainly, this was because of the situation in the labour market. Although unemployment rates were higher than ever, it was surprisingly difficult for the car industry to find new workers. Between March 1975 and December 1976, the personnel department at Opel Rüsselsheim offered about 22,600 applicants jobs as manual workers; only 69 per cent accepted. By the end of 1976, less than two-thirds (63 per cent) of the new entrants were still in employment; the rest had resigned. Of the 13,700 Germans who had been offered manual jobs, no more than 65 per cent accepted, and of those only 54 per cent were still at Opel by December 1976. Recruitment was less difficult with foreign workers and least difficult with workers from non-EEC countries (mostly Turks and Greeks). In this group, 82 per cent of the 5,400 who were offered a job accepted, and 83 per cent of those who took up work were still in employment by the end of the period. The problem was, however, that in response to the increasing general unemployment, the government had banned the recruitment of workers from outside the EEC who were not already living in Germany. As a result, the labour market for a company like Opel was, contrary to appearances, extremely tight.

With the new car boom running high, and the chances of a 'solidaristic' policy against unemployment limited by the structure of the labour market, the Opel works council between August 1975 and September 1976 lapsed back into a normal pattern of surreptitious supplementary bargaining. As shown in Table 7.2 on four occasions during the thirteen months the works council agreed to overtime shifts in exchange for various material concessions. Among the concessions gained, the additional break negotiated in August 1975 was regarded as particularly important by the works council. In January 1976, the two sides agreed on a further break of 10 minutes, this time for every eight hours worked regardless of temperature. Finally, in June 1976 another break, also of 10 minutes, was negotiated for hot days. As a result,

Table 7.2   Agreements on overtime shifts between works council and management at Opel Rüsselsheim

August, 1975: Six shifts

(i)   No dismissals for lack of work until March 1976

(ii)   No short-time work until February 1976

(iii)   An additional break (10 minutes) for production workers on each day with an outside temperature of more than 30°C

(iv)   Further fixed-term contracts are changed into regular employment contracts

September, 1975: Six shifts

(i)   No dismissals for lack of work until June, 1976

(ii)   No short-time work until March, 1976

(iii)   Overtime shift bonus increased to DM 15

(iv)   December 24 and 31 become paid holidays

(v)   The remaining fixed-term contracts are changed into regular employment contracts

January, 1976: Eight shifts

(i)   An additional break (10 minutes) per working day for production workers

(ii)   Improved conditions for workers buying Opel cars (saving of DM 90–250 per car)

(iii)   Works agreement ruling out fixed-term contracts for the future

April, 1976: Eight shifts

(i)   Wages(a) increased by 5.4 per cent (industrial agreement: 4 per cent)

(ii)   Higher bonuses for piece rate work

(iii)   One more paid holiday

(iv)   Works agreement ruling out dismissals for five months

(a) Existing Opel wages, which at this time were about 25 per cent higher than required by the industrial agremeent.

production workers on such days had five per cent of their working time as 'personal time' (24 minutes), the 10-minute break negotiated in January 1976 and two breaks of 10 minutes each for high temperatures – 54 minutes in all.

In the four months from June to September 1975, production workers at Opel Rüsselsheim worked altogether 12 overtime shifts. On the average, each worker spent 12 additional hours per month at work which amounted to roughly a 43-hour week. Increasingly, this was seen by many workers as excessive. In response to the changing mood among its electorate, the works council in late 1975 formally resolved that in the future it would not agree to more than two overtime shifts (one for each individual worker) per month. As a consequence, the number of overtime shifts in the 11 months from October 1975 to August 1976 did not exceed 26, and the average monthly number per production worker fell to less than 1.2

Third round: 'black September'

In September 1976, the works council saw a chance to return to its original, more principled attitude on overtime. When approached by management for another four overtime shifts, the works council argued that the workforce was overworked. In particular, it pointed out that this applied not only to the production workers but also to the maintenance workers who had been working most Saturday afternoons and sometimes even on Sundays. Furthermore, the works council maintained that the cars produced during the overtime shifts would be used to replenish dealers' stocks and thus prepare the way for short-time work in the future.

However, rather than just rejecting the management's request, the works council responded by making a counter-demand. In return for the four overtime shifts, the company was asked to establish a special income maintenance fund for short-time workers. For each overtime shift worked, the company was to pay a certain amount into the fund. The money was to be used to pay workers the difference between their normal take-home pay and the benefits received during short-time work.

The demand for an income maintenance fund was another attempt to create a linkage between overtime and short-time work. To the workers it was presented primarily in terms of its expected positive effects on their income. Its real purpose, however, was to make both overtime and short-time work more expensive for the company and thereby force it to 'even out' the cycles in its use of labour. After the establishment of the fund, it was hoped that the management would have one more, and perhaps a decisive, financial incentive to plan the company's labour input more carefully. The expected and desired result was a reduction not only of overtime but also of short-time work.

According to calculations made by the works council, compensating an average production worker for his or her loss of income during one week of short-time work in 1976 would have cost the company about DM 60 per worker. The works council suggested that this amount should be distributed over two overtime shifts so that for each worker showing up for an overtime shift, the company would pay DM 30 into the income maintenance fund. To be insured against the loss of income resulting from 13 weeks of short-time work – as many as had occurred during the critical period between late 1973 and early 1975 – a worker would thus have to work 26 overtime shifts (the company as a whole, 52). The total cost of income maintenance for 20,000 production workers in Rüsselsheim and 15,000 in Bochum during 13 weeks of short-time work would be DM 27.3 million. The works council argued that this was not much. In 1976, the company had made a profit of DM 730 million; 27.3 million was no more than four per cent of this sum.

The main reason why the management found the income maintenance fund unacceptable was not its cost – although, of course, the amount to be paid into the fund for an overtime shift was likely to increase in the future as a result of further works council demands. Whether or not the fund would have forced the management to change its policies on overtime and short-time work is difficult to say; from the relatively low amounts of money involved, it seems more likely that it would not. At the time the management was more concerned about the effect the scheme might have on morale. If, as is frequently the case, not all workers in a particular department are put on short-time work – what incentive would there be for the others to work if short-time workers suffered no financial loss? In the end, it could have become necessary to pay an extra bonus to those who were not laid off – or, as suggested by the works council, to organise a complicated, and hardly reliable, rotation system.

In an attempt to improve its bargaining position, the Rüsselsheim works council had persuaded its counterpart at Bochum to join in the demand for an income maintenance fund. Although in the ensuing weeks of talks the two bodies co-ordinated their actions closely, the result was a political disaster. At Rüsselsheim, the events were later commonly referred to by the works council as 'our black September'. When confronted with the two works councils' response, the management unexpectedly made no offer at all but immediately called for conciliation. Two committees were set up, one for each plant. No compromise was reached during the proceedings and the chairmen had to cast their votes. In Bochum, the chairman voted with the management in support of its original request for four overtime shifts. In Rüsselsheim, where the works council seems to have argued its case against overtime more effectively, the chairman first voted with the works council against four shifts, but then voted with the management for two shifts.

At first glance, this result, as far as Rüsselsheim was concerned, could well appear as a partial success, and so it was indeed perceived by the public. Although the ambitious goal of income maintenance for short-time workers had not been realised – but had gained considerable publicity – a first step seemed to have been made to end the management's excessive use of overtime and protect the health and family life of the workers. However, this was not the way the two works councils could afford to see the matter. For them, and even more so for their constituents, the important point was that as a result of the committee's award, the company had got overtime without the workforce getting anything in return.

Moreover, from the perspective of the Rüsselsheim production workers, the fact that they had been ordered to work two shifts less than their counterparts at Bochum meant that their income in the following weeks would be about DM 300 lower. The situation was exacerbated by the fact that in advance of the conciliation committee decision, the two works councils had reached agreement with the management on a thirteenth monthly wage to be paid as a Christmas bonus. The bonus was to be calculated on the basis of a worker's total yearly pay including overtime. As a consequence of the different conciliation awards, production workers in Rüsselsheim were therefore not only to get a substantially lower income from overtime but also a lower Christmas bonus.

There was no doubt on the part of the Rüsselsheim works council that they could not simply accept their defeat and return to normal business. The situation demanded an unmistakable demonstration of political resolve – not only to save face with the workforce and the union activists but also, and in particular, to show the management that further attempts to get overtime through conciliation rather than negotiation would not be tolerated. Immediately after the conciliation committee had made its award, the works council imposed an indefinite ban on overtime except for the two shifts ordered by the committee. To implement the ban, works council procedures were changed so that every single request by the management for overtime, however small the number of workers concerned, was to be decided by the full council. Since the works council recognised that there were cases in which it was impossible to refuse overtime – for example, in emergencies – each request had to be considered in detail. Frequently, requests were supported by the works council member in charge of the department from which they came, and to the extent that such requests were rejected by majority vote on the works council relations between works councillors themselves became increasingly strained. More and more, the old factional divisions reappeared. Almost all of the works council's time and political attention were devoted to discussions on overtime. It was obvious to everybody that this could not continue forever. But the expectation of management that the works council would either break apart or lose the support of the workforce – especially of the foreign workers – turned out to be mistaken. Although many workers would have liked to work overtime, the works council's strategy of confrontation was approved by a day-long works meeting.

After this, management began to make advances to resolve the deadlock without loss of face for the works council. When the management suggested a new formula for the calculation of the Christmas bonus which gave production workers in Rüsselsheim as much as in Bochum, the general overtime ban was finally lifted.

Fourth round: repercussions in the IGM

After the 'black September' episode, frustration among union activists at Opel Rüsselheim ran high. Internal discussions during the following weeks focused on the perennial problem of the integration of the car industry, and of Opel in particular, into the industrial agreement for the engineering industry. Many at Opel felt that the conciliation committee affair had once again proved the impossibility of correcting the deficiencies of industry-wide collective bargaining by conventional means and within the legal framework of co-determination. The industrial agreement in the spring had remained far below what Opel could have afforded to pay. Although the 'general wage round' had been relatively successful, the company's profits were still exceptionally high and continued to rise. In this situation, the fate of the income maintenance fund was taken by many as proof that the existing system of collective bargaining made it impossible for workers in companies like Opel to get their fair share. It was in this context that the idea of an autonomous car industry trade group within IGM came to be seriously considered by some union representatives at Opel in December 1976.

Although after the event, attempts were made to blame the reopening of the trade group discussion on the left faction, when the idea was first brought up it was by a member of the right-wing group during a *Vertrauensleute* meeting. Later, its proponents seem to have come from both the right and the left. The crucial and politically sensitive point was the suggestion that the trade group should negotiate a separate industrial agreement for the car industry. In late December, the press became aware of the development, and the *Frankfurter Rundschau* reported on it in a long article.

For the works council leadership, this development created difficult political problems. Although the leaders themselves had their doubts on the existing institutional framework of collective bargaining, they did not support the trade group proposal, and they in fact tried from the beginning to prevent it being further discussed. In their view, the idea of a separate car unit in IGM negotiating a separate industrial agreement was totally unrealistic. Given the existing political and organisational structure in IGM, the only way a special car industry agreement could be achieved would be by organising a breakaway car workers union. Since the Opel works council was neither able nor, for that matter, willing to do this, it was in its best interest to avoid the appearance of being associated with plans of this kind. The article in the *Frankfurter Rundschau* was all the more embarrassing since it appeared on the eve of the Böblingen conference (see p. 118) – the same occasion at which the works council intended to express its misgivings on the union's wage policy and on what it regarded as lack of support on the income maintenance fund. The talk in the Rüsselsheim plant about a car industry trade group provided the national leadership with a welcome opportunity to accuse the Rüsselsheim works council of 'unsolidaristic' and divisive tendencies and thus to discredit whatever substantive points they might want to make.

To bring the discussion of a car industry trade group to an end, the leaders of the works council majority suggested that Opel workers should try to obtain a majority in the union for an 'opening clause' to be inserted in the industrial agreement for the engineering industry. The clause would enable union workplace organisations in prospering firms – such as Opel – to conduct an official 'second wage round' and, in particular, to call a strike in support of their additional demands. The advantage for the works council would be that it would no longer have to use its co-determination rights on matters like overtime to top up the industrial agreement; instead, it could use them for more workplace-specific purposes, such as an improvement of working conditions. (As a works council member put it in a later interview, 'The way things are now, we have to give away overtime shifts for a higher Christmas bonus or better piece rates. But we would rather use them to make the company install air conditioning'.)

However, the fact that they had directed the discontent in their organisation into more conventional channels did not help the Opel leaders much at Böblingen. From the beginning, the discussion centred on the events reported in the newspaper article. In his opening address, Loderer himself took up the matter, stating that he considered any proposal of separate industrial agreements for individual industries an attempt to split up the union, and that such tendencies had to be fought with all means and at all costs. Among those who in the course of the debate attacked the Opel leadership most heavily were members of the Volkswagen works council. For the Opel delegation, this was ironic since Volkswagen with its company agreement just did not have many of the problems which had led to the political developments in the Opel union organisation. When they felt that not even their more orthodox demand for opening clauses received a fair hearing, the Opel delegation changed the subject and brought up the overtime problem. In particular, they compared their record of resistance to overtime to the 'middle-line manpower policy' at Volkswagen, maintaining that while they had been struggling to reduce overtime in order to create additional employment, the Volkswagen council had been collaborating with the management to keep the workforce small. In effect, they maintained, the IGM at Volkswagen contributed to unemployment. The Opel delegates moved that the conference endorse as official union policy that works councils should refuse overtime and instead urge their companies to employ more workers. In the end, no vote was taken, and the issue remained undecided.

To an important extent, the Böblingen conference was used by the participants as a testing ground for the triennial IGM general conference which was due to be held in September 1977. During the summer, the IGM Rüsselsheim district (which is dominated by the Opel workers) prepared a resolution demanding that future industrial agreements should have opening clauses. After a lengthy debate at the general conference in which several Opel works councillors took the floor, the motion was defeated by a margin of about 9 to 1. Most of the delegates were either full-time officers or works councillors, and while the first were opposed to opening clauses because they had no interest in workplace organisations gaining more independence, the second preferred to negotiate the benefits of the 'second wage round' themselves rather than have them negotiated by the union. To the works councillors in particular, the Opel leaders in demanding opening clauses acted against their own institutional interests, and this was perceived by many as an indication of a fundamental lack of practical experience. With hindsight, the Opel leaders themselves tend to see their behaviour in these terms. As the works council chairman put it in an interview, the debate at the 1977 general conference convinced him that the union would never accept opening clauses of the kind he had proposed, and he would in future refrain from 'antagonizing everybody' in the union by trying to give away prerogatives which apparently nobody wanted to have.

Fifth round: back to traditional supplementary bargaining
Immediately after the Böblingen conference, the 1977 wage round moved into its final phase. When the union set up its initial demands, the Opel delegates on the IGM negotiating committee for the Land of Hesse pressed without success for a flat rate rather than a percentage

wage increase. In late February, agreement was reached to increase wages by between 6.9 and 7.1 per cent in the major wage grades; for the lowest grade, the increase was to be 8.2 per cent. When shortly after this the Opel works council was approached by management for six more overtime shifts, it decided to use this as an opportunity to realise at least in part the objectives of its original flat rate proposal.

In the ensuing negotiations on the 'application' of the industrial agreement, the works council got the management to apply the percentage increases provided for under the agreement to the full wages paid at Opel including wage drift. In addition, it was agreed that workers in the three lowest grades should get the same absolute money increases as workers in the fourth-lowest grade. This benefited primarily the production workers. Thus, while workers in the highest grade got the official increase of 6.9 per cent, those in the lowest grade got 9 per cent; the percentage increase for the other grades lay between these and became higher the lower the wage grade. A similar agreement was reached for salaried staff. The effect was still higher wage drift especially in the middle and lower grades and a reduction of the differential between the highest and the lowest grade from 60 to 57 per cent. For the works council, this outcome was of great political significance. It could be drawn upon to demonstrate that supplementary bargaining could be used not just to top up an official wage increase but also to change the wage structure in accordance with egalitarian values not supported by official union policy. In return, the works council agreed to the six requested overtime shifts.

Sixth round: failure of the income maintenance fund
When in May 1977 the management asked for another six overtime shifts, the works council renewed its demand for an income maintenance scheme for workers on short time. In part, this was with an eye to the forthcoming IGM general conference for which the Opel leaders wanted to keep the overtime issue alive. The external conditions appeared favourable. By that time, the Social Democratic Party, the Labour Ministry, the DGB and even IGM headquarters had discovered the possibility of creating new jobs through a reduction of overtime – or at least they were paying lip service to the idea. As far as Opel was concerned, the works council could point to the fact that in their plant for the last two years the Saturday morning shift had been the rule rather than the exception. In effect, this meant that the 40-hour-week had been abandoned and thus arguably Opel was in breach of the industrial agreement. Moreover, for some groups of skilled maintenance workers a case could be made that the Working Hours Regulation which is an official statute had been constantly violated during the period. In a press interview during the talks on the income maintenance

fund, the chairman of the Bochum works council characterised this situation by the often-quoted sentence: 'We are producing not only cars but also cripples.'

On the other hand, the management also had some points in its favour. By April 1977, the Rüsselsheim workforce had reached 36,000 and thus was almost as large as before the crisis of February 1973. Furthermore, the difficulties of finding workers willing to work in the car industry had not eased in spite of rising unemployment. There were good reasons for the management to expect that if the matter went to conciliation, the company's employment record and its problems on the labour market would not fail to impress the chairman. In its response to the management's request for the six overtime shifts, the works council had asked for two things: the income maintenance fund and an additional paid holiday. Both demands were refused. When after several rounds of talks nothing had moved on either side, it was agreed to set up a conciliation committee. A professor of labour law who was known to be an expert on the Works Constitution Act was appointed chairman. In its presentation to the committee the works council, as one minor point among others, mentioned that there might have been a violation of the Working Hours Regulation. To its surprise, and probably to that of the management as well, the chairman immediately seized on this subject and began an extensive enquiry into it. While the works council did not object, it felt that this was 'extremely formalistic' and betrayed 'complete lack of practical experience'. Although it had been the works council itself which had raised the matter, it had done so for formal reasons and on the assumption that everybody knew that in practice 'the Regulation is violated every day' – and frequently with the assent of the works council. As one of the works council representatives later put it, 'only a law professor could get so excited about this.'

In several consecutive sessions the management had to answer the chairman's queries on the company's compliance with the Working Hours Regulation. To bring this to an end the management, in informal talks with the works council, suddenly offered to concede the additional paid holiday. This was not accepted, however, partly because the income maintenance fund had by this time received so much publicity that the works council could not simply drop its demand and partly because the works council had gained the impression that the conciliation proceedings were running in its favour. This impression was obviously shared by management which felt that its dubious compliance with the law on working hours had turned the chairman against it. After its compromise proposal had been refused, the management withdrew its request for the six overtime shifts and thereby brought the conciliation proceedings to an abrupt end.

In many ways, the resulting situation has even more unpleasant for the works council than the 'black September' episode. It had failed to get both the additional holiday and the income maintenance fund. While the refusal of the income maintenance fund did not come as a complete surprise, the works council had hoped for a majority vote by the committee declaring that such a demand was within the law; this would have given it additional respectability. The matter could then have gone to the Labour Court where it would have been resolved one way or another. Instead, because of the chairman's fascination with the Working Hours Regulation, the legal merits of the works council's case remained untested.

That the works council had been able to prevent further overtime shifts did not offer much consolation. Although in public it was once more acclaimed for its 'solidaristic' behaviour and its successful defence of the workers' 'real' interests, quite a few of the workers themselves saw the matter differently. To them, the outstanding result of the works council's tactics was that they had gained neither the additional holiday nor the income maintenance fund. In addition, they had been deprived of the opportunity to increase their income through overtime. To make things worse, shortly after the dissolution of the conciliation committee, the management let the works council know that from now on, formal applications for overtime shifts would be made only if the works council indicated in advance that they would not be opposed on principle. Since the works council would not yield, not a single over-time shift was requested during the entire summer. As a consequence, the works council's bargaining power declined sharply. With one of its most important commodities no longer in demand, the capacity of the works council to extract concessions from management became mini-mal. Thus, after May 1977 company supplementary bargaining at Opel Rüsselsheim came to an almost complete standstill.

In September Opel could no longer avoid the publication of its balance sheet. When they learned about the company's record profits, the *Vertrauensleute* urged the works council to take action to secure a share for the workers. By this time in the year, the negotiations on the Christmas bonus should have long been underway, but since the man-agement had stopped asking for overtime shifts, there had been no opportunity for the works council to get them going. When the impasse threatened to continue, the works council finally took the initiative and wrote a letter to the management; the letter contained a long list of specific demands. In response, the management indicated that it was in principle prepared to negotiate. It also expressed an interest in six overtime shifts. After informal talks, agreement was reached on an additional Christmas bonus of DM 400 for everybody on top of the thirteenth monthly wage. Furthermore, as envisaged at the time of the conciliation committee proceedings, December 30 was made a paid holiday. In return, the works council agreed to the six overtime shifts. Since the agreement represented a retreat from the earlier more principled policy on overtime, it was formally concluded only after a positive vote in the assembly of *Vertrauensleute*.

Apart from the need to resuscitate the normal bargaining process, the works council had concluded that the income maintenance fund was unacceptable to management on principle ('an ideological question') and that it was impossible to get it with the means available to a works council. When IGM in the autumn of 1977 began to prepare the following year's wage round, the Opel delegates on the Hesse negotiating committee moved that the union include the income maintenance fund for short-time workers among its demands. This would have made it possible to call a strike to support the demand. However, the proposal was rejected. To most other members of the negotiating committee, the fund was 'a typical Opel problem' or even just the personal whim of the chairman of the Opel works council. Moreover, the majority of the committee members were works council leaders themselves who found it not in their interest to raise the costs of overtime for employers through an industrial agreement and thus constrain negotiations on overtime at the company level.

After the fund had been voted down by the committee, the leaders of the Rüsselsheim works council felt free to drop their proposal from their political agenda. In this, they were supported by growing doubts in the public on the possible effectiveness of a reduction of overtime as a way of creating new jobs. Ever more frequently, the point was made that only a minor proportion of the unemployed were able or willing to fill the vacancies that might be created by restrictions on overtime. In any case, the matter was now contested between the parties forming the government coalition, and no political action in this direction was to be expected.

By the end of the year, the original optimism of the new Rüsselsheim works council majority on the possibility of steady income and employment in the car industry had disappeared. In an interview conducted for this study, a leading member of the works council admitted that in times of declining demand, short-time work might be inevitable. While the works council had to do its utmost to keep the use of labour 'as steady as possible', there was no sense in objecting to overtime or short-time work as a matter of principle – not least because refusing overtime for ideological reasons would inevitably bring defeat in the next works council election. (At the time of the interview, the campaign for the 1978 works council election – in which the incumbent leadership was returned with a wide margin – was already under way.)

Also, in retrospect, the works council believed that they had failed to pay sufficient attention to the political risks of forcing the employer to take on new workers during a boom. In a subsequent recession, the management might have to approach the works council for short-time work or dismissals, and the works council might have to negotiate a redundancy scheme and participate in its implementation. 'To be frank, these things we have just refused to think about.' In effect, then, at the end of 1977, the 'radical' works council at Opel and the 'conservative' one at Volkswagen, however contrasting their positions may have appeared to the public, not only followed the same policy of permitting no more, and no less, than two overtime shifts per month; they also were in basic agreement on the possibilities and the limits of a works council trying to influence its employer's manpower policy.

Note on sources

The case studies in Chapters 5, 6 and 7 are based on a variety of sources. First and foremost, they draw on a number of interviews with works councillors at Wolfsburg and Rüsselsheim and with union officials from IGM headquarters.

Secondly, information has been collected from the official publications of the parties involved, notably from the circular of the Wolfsburg central works council, *BR Aktuell*, the IGM monthly, *Der Gewierk-scafter*, the IGM business report 1974–76, and the Volkswagen business reports for 1970 to 1976.

Furthermore, the IGM press office kindly provided the author with complete collections of newspaper clippings that were prepared for internal use on the following subjects: the 1976 Volkswagen redundancy scheme, the Volkswagen decision on the US plant, and the controversy on overtime at Volkswagen.

Finally, the author has profited from a number of book and journal articles, in particular from Rainer Dombois, Massenentlassungen bei VW: Individualisierung der Krise, *Leviathan*, 4 (1976), pp.432–63 and Gunter Wallraff, Volkswagen: Eine Konzernstrategie und ihre Folgen, in R. Duhm and H. Wieser, eds., *Krise und Gegenwehr*, (Berlin, 1977), pp. 80–99.

Footnotes

[1] It is possible, of course, to define part of the normal working week as overtime to justify higher pay. In the present discussion, the term 'overtime' is limited to additional working time added to normal working hours on a temporary irregular basis.

[2] This distinction corresponds roughly to 'unskilled' and 'skilled' workers in the British car industry.

[3] Overtime for non-productive workers is organised differently. In this group overtime is normally worked in the form of additional hours, not on an additional working day.

[4] Since overtime pay is taxed at a lower rate than normal pay in Germany, the

increase in take-home pay was even higher.

5 'Social considerations' is an inadequate translation of the German term *'Soziale Gesichtspunkte*! The term refers to the characteristics of a person that entitle him or her to special protection. *Soziale Gesichtspunkte* that may have to be considered in dismissals are a person's marital status, age, family income, and so on.

6 In German car factories, workers are entitled under works agreements to buy a car at a reduced price every one or two years depending mainly on their seniority (*Jahreswagen*). When workers get a new car, they sell their last one at approximately the price they paid for it. Daimler-Benz workers normally get more for their *Jahreswagen* than they would cost new at the dealers, the reason being that delivery terms for Mercedes cars are so long that customers are prepared to pay more to get a car immediately even if it has already been used for one year. This system constitutes an important part of a car worker's income and especially at Daimler-Benz. It is viewed with great displeasure by the dealers.

7 In 1977, 64,000 Volkswagens were sold at reduced prices to Volkswagen workers. In 1973 the number was 34,000.

8 There are two Opel plants in Germany: Rüsselsheim (which is the older one) and Bochum. The Bochum plant is smaller than the one at Rüsselsheim. In this case study, a reference to Opel means the Rüsselsheim plant unless otherwise indicated.

9 The central works council at Opel has much less power over the works councils of individual plants than its counterpart at Volkswagen. Partly, this is because Opel has only two plants which are of almost equal size and also the management of the company is not highly centralised. Furthermore, while at Volkswagen all plants are subject to one (company) labour agreement, the two Opel plants are located in different negotiating areas of IGM (Hesse and North-Rhine-Westphalia) with different industrial agreements. Not least, the representation of workers on the Opel supervisory board does not exceed the legal limit for companies outside the coal and steel industry and there is only one shareholder which is a private foreign company (General Motors). This reduces both the chances for the union to use the supervisory board as a mechanism of interest representation and the role of the chairman of the central works council as a member of the supervisory board.

8 Some Tentative Conclusions

Systems of industrial relations are institutionalised arrangements for the representation and accommodation of the interests of participants in the labour market. Interest representation, in industry as well as in other spheres of social life, can be organised and linked into the polity at large in a variety of ways. To characterise and classify differently structured systems of interest representation, political scientists have in recent years increasingly made use of the distinction between 'pluralism' and 'corporatism'. According to Schmitter,[1] corporatist systems of interest representation differ from pluralist ones by their more orderly and planned structure as well as their more intimate, and more dependent, relationship with the State. In particular, pluralism and corporatism are distinguished in the following way:

Pluralism		Corporatism
	(is) a system of interest representation in which the constituent units are organised into an	
unspecified		*limited*
	number of	
multiple		*singular*
voluntary		*compulsory*
competitive		*non-competitive*
non-hierarchically ordered		*hierarchically ordered*
self-determined (as to type or scope of interests		*functionally differentiated*
	categories which are	
not specially licensed recognised, subsidised, created or otherwise controlled in leadership selection		*recognised or licensed (if not created)*
	by the State	
and which do not exercise a monopoly of representational activity within their respective categories		*and granted a deliberate representational monopoly within their respective categories in exchange for observing certain controls on their selection of leaders and articulation of demands*(2)

There is no reason to expect that any empirical system of interest representation will completely meet the definition of either pluralism or corporatism. Both concepts are ideal types, and one might conceive of them as of the end-points of a continuum, with most or all systems being located somewhere between them. On the other hand, looking at the British and the German industrial relations systems, it could be said that they fall neatly into the two categories. The British system comes fairly close to the pluralist end of the continuum, while the German system exhibits important traits of the corporatist type. Thus:

(a)   the number of interest categories which get access to collective representation in the German system is limited by the Works Constitution Act and the Collective Agreements Act (*Tarifvertragsgesetz*). While the former concentrates workplace bargaining at the level of the undertaking as a whole, the latter facilitates industry-wide bargaining. Moreover and partly as a consequence of this, there are only a small number of unions, and these are of large size and internally heterogeneous. In Britain, by way of contrast, the number and structure of bargaining units is not restricted or constrained by external regulation and, especially in the private sector, depends exclusively on voluntary arrangements between unions and employers, and trade unions are numerous, fragmented and specialised;

(b)   the interests of workers in a specific trade or industry in Germany are represented by the same union throughout the country (unit singularity) while in Britain they may be represented by different unions in different places (unit multiplicity);

(c)   representation at the workplace through the works council in Germany is on a statutory basis and therefore compulsory. As has been shown, there are certain mechanisms through which compulsory representation by works councils is transformed into *de facto* compulsory membership of trade unions. In Britain, by comparison, there is no compulsory representation based on statute, and closed shops are strictly private in the sense that they have to be agreed upon case by case between unions and employers (the decisive factor being the specific distribution of power). Thus although there is compulsory union membership in Britain, the British industrial relations system is rightly considered the prime example of a voluntary structure;

(d)   there is no, or only negligible, inter-union competition in Germany while there is a considerable amount of such competition in Britain;

(e)   bargaining arenas in Germany are hierarchically ordered in the sense that industrial agreements take legal precedence over workplace agreements (*Betriebsvereinbarungen*) and the collective bargaining system as a whole is subject to legal control and enforcement. In Britain, no such hierarchical ordering exists, and where it does – for example, in certain procedure agreements – it is much easier to circumvent and frustrate;

(f) there is a clearly established differentiation in Germany between the functions of different categories of interest representatives, for example, union steward, works councillors, the industrial union, even though this differentiation of function is sometimes ignored. In Britain, on the other hand, it is left exclusively to the participants in a particular bargaining arena to determine the type or scope of the interests about which they wish to bargain (this is less so in the public sector);

(g) State licensing of interest associations takes various forms in the German system centring around the enforceability of industrial agreements and works agreements and the extension by law of collective agreements to non-members of the associations that have concluded an agreement. While works councils are constituted under the direct control of the law, trade unions are formally, and to a great extent factually, independent of the State. On the other hand, the Works Constitution Act and the Collective Agreements Act in effect exclude certain types of unions (for example, small, specialised ones) from collective bargaining and in this sense indirectly license the large industrial unions. The legal institutional framework also makes 'market access' for newly formed organisations exceedingly difficult. In Britain, on the other hand, the system of industrial relations is almost entirely free from State interference and it is exempt from the common law;

(h) works councils in Germany do have a legal monopoly of representation over a certain range of subjects, and in exchange for this they have to observe a general peace obligation. Industrial unions, with few exceptions, also are representational monopolists, and this is partly due to the various covert mechanisms of state licensing and partly to the fact that the works councils system favours broad-based industrial unions over sectional unions. The notion of a State-guaranteed or State-supported monopoly of representation for unions or employers associations is alien in the British context.

Although the distinction between pluralism and corporatism refers to institutional structures rather than policies, it derives its relevance from the relationship between structure and policy. To clarify this relationship as it applies to industrial relations systems, it is useful to refer back to Mancur Olson's theory of the 'political economy of economic growth rates' (see Chapter 1). The organisation of interests in a limited number of large, internally heterogenous units, a characteristic of corporatism by definition, is obviously identical with what Olson refers to as 'encompassing organisations'. Correspondingly, what Olson describes as the 'natural' pattern of interest organisation – the fragmentation of interests into narrow, highly specific, sectional associations – is what in recent theories of interest representation has been called a pluralist structure. If Olson's theory about the different attitudes of small and large, exclusive and inclusive, specialised and comprehensive associations towards the interests and functional requirements of the economy as a whole are correct, *ceteris paribus* economies with a corporatist system of industrial relations would be expected to perform better than economies with a pluralist industrial relations system.

The same result is arrived at through yet another line of reasoning. In corporatist systems, interests are not only combined *horizontally* into large encompassing aggregates but are also *vertically* organised into various hierarchically related levels of aggregation. This makes them much more accessible to central co-ordination and concentration. To the extent that economic performance depends on sectional industrial interests being prevented from seeking realisation at the expense of general interests such as a high level of productivity, corporatist systems of industrial relations are likely to be more successful economically than pluralist systems whose hierarchical dimension is less developed or non-existent. While in a corporatist system the temptation of sectional interest groups to take advantage of the community at large can be checked by powerful actors representing a more aggregate interest perspective, this does not apply in a pluralist system where the limits of sectional action are defined by the market in the widest sense rather than by a hierarchy. In this way corporatist systems are said to be more governable, and corporatist industrial relations more manageable, than pluralist systems. The effect of the existence of a hierarchical control capacity is reinforced by the fact that the units of action in corporatist systems are more encompassing than in pluralist ones – which makes them voluntarily articulate only those interests which are already comparatively close to the general interest. In other words, while corporatist systems do have a capacity to constrain their constituent units in the general interest, these units by themselves internalise many of their interests and, in addition to performing important functions of interest accommodation internally and on their own, are more easily accessible than pluralist ones to concertation by external co-ordinating agencies such as the State.

The policy outcomes of corporatist institutions of industrial relations have in the past been discussed primarily in terms of incomes policy and the struggle against inflation. There are indeed indications that attempts at a joint regulation of incomes at the level of the national economy are more likely to succeed if industrial interests are organised in a corporatist rather than a pluralist fashion. On the other hand, the general preoccupation in recent years with the demand side of the economy has tended to hide the fact that corporatist structures of interest intermediation perform at least as important functions on the supply side as they do in the regulation of aggregate demand. It could even be said that where a concerted incomes policy was or is successful, this is to an important degree because of the positive effect corporatist institutions have on the organisation of production, and where as in Germany this effect is sufficiently strong, concertation of demand seems to work even in the absence of a formalised 'Concerted Action'.

The way corporatist institutions of industrial relations affect the supply side of the economic process has been outlined in general terms by Olson. Corporatist systems of industrial relations exclude from articulation sectional interests that stand to profit from preservation of the *status quo* in spite of resulting sub-optimal performance of the industry or economy. Because of the way corporatist organisations aggregate, process and transform the interests of their members, they allow for a good deal of flexibility of the productive apparatus and a high rate of efficient adjustment and restructuring. As far as the joint regulation of the use of labour (or manpower policy) is concerned, corporatist interest organisation contributes to industrial flexibility by excluding from representation demands of negatively affected member groups for job control and job ownership, and by permitting a high degree of mobility of labour within and between plants. Pluralist systems, on the other hand, give small groups in a strong bargaining position a chance to establish defensive veto rights over changes in the organisation of their work and thus obstruct industrial adjustment to the detriment of the industry or economy as a whole. The result may be a lasting interest-political deadlock leading to and accompanied by economic stagnation and decline which compares unfavourably with the capacity of corporatist industrial relations systems for concerted and negotiated adaptation.

The present study has presented two examples of negotiated/concerted industrial restructuring in a corporatist system of interest intermediation. In the first case – the reduction of the Volkswagen workforce by 20,000 workers in 1975 – an economically viable solution was reached for a critical over-capacity problem without industrial disruptions and without union and employer combining to extract subsidies from the public. Among the factors that made it possible for the West German government to hold on to its non-protectionist policy were, as already demonstrated in detail, the comprehensiveness and the monopolistic position of IGM as an industrial union representing all categories of workers in the German engineering industry; the hierarchical control capacity of the union leadership over the works council, and the respective capacity of the central works council over the local works councils, and of the latter over the union stewards at the workplace; the legal limitations on the works councils' range of actions; and the institutionalisation in law of the union as a responsible participant in the company's decision-making process through co-determination. The solution that was worked out after long negotiations was far less costly for the economy than continued stagnation financed by the taxpayer, and it would have kept Volkswagen in business even if the 1975 car boom had come later and more slowly. Similar considerations apply to the second case, the decision to build a Volkswagen assembly plant in the United States. Although case studies can never be conclusive, and although other factors have undoubtedly also played a role, the two examples seem to present strong *prima facie* evidence for the thesis that the form in which industrial interests are organised does make a difference, and that corporatist interest organisation indeed facilitates industrial restructuring and thus contributes to economic performance.

In the remainder of this chapter, three of the many questions raised by the theories already introduced will be considered. The first question concerns the origin of institutional differences such as those existing between Britain and Germany that apparently have such far-reaching consequences for a country's economic performance. On this point, Olson offers an interesting hypothesis, and this will be examined. The problem of 'transferability' will then be considered. If inclusive, corporatist institutions of industrial interest representation can help to improve economic performance, it may be important in a country that does not have such institutions to know whether and to what extent it can deliberately create them. Finally, there will be a more systematic discussion of the assertion that corporatist industrial relations systems are economically more successful than pluralist ones. In particular, it will be discussed whether the alleged superiority of corporatist systems obtains under all circumstances or only under specific conditions that are subject to change.

Interest representation and the problem of institutional arthritis
Why is it that a country like Great Britain has a fragmented, decentralised and sectional interest group structure while the corresponding structure in West Germany is comprehensive, centralised and encompassing? Olson's answer is, in essence, that as a result of a general 'logic of the formation of organised groups, democratic countries with freedom of organisation gradually accumulate powerful common-interest organisations' which, among other things, adversely affect the economy's flexibility and growth rate. In this sense, democratic societies are subject to a creeping disease which Olson calls 'institutional arthritis' (and which he identifies with what is commonly called the 'English disease'). The development of this condition is interrupted, and its results are undone, only by catastrophic breakdowns of a country's institutional continuity – such as a conquest by a foreign power. After

such catastrophies, only few group interests continue to be organised, and their claims to power and influence are no longer established. During the considerable time it takes for organised group interests to re-emerge and re-establish themselves, countries that have suffered an institutional breakdown are able to show better economic performance and have higher growth rates than countries with long historical continuity. Olson's principal examples of the first category of countries are Japan, West Germany and Italy after the second world war while his foremost example for the second category is, of course, Great Britain.

At first glance, this theory sounds both familiar and plausible. It has often been argued in Britain that the grand simplicity of the West German trade union system is due to the unique historical opportunity the Germans had after the defeat in 1945 to organise their union movement in a new, much more comprehensive and inclusive pattern. The advantage of Olson's paper is that it reveals some of the general assumptions that underly such historicist reasoning. One of them is that interest-political pluralism is a function of time – that it is the more pronounced the older the institutional system and the more uninterrupted growth it has experienced. Put in this explicit form, the argument does not look very convincing, and a number of counter-arguments can be made. For example, it is true that German trade unionism before 1933 had a more complex organisational structure than it has now, but the differences are far less dramatic than the *tabula rasa* theory of German industrial unionism after 1945 would make them appear. In particular, trade unionism in Germany was always much less fragmented and much more centralised than in Britain, before 1933 no less than after 1945. Moreover, the structure of West German trade unionism during the history of the Federal Republic has, if anything, become more rather than less centralised and inclusive. Even in Britain the number of trade unions, including those not affiliated to the TUC, has declined over time (from 704 unions inside and outside the TUC in 1955, to 454 in 1979).

Even more telling is the case of another country, Sweden, which Olson himself mentions as one which he finds difficult to account for. Sweden, after the second world war, had a 'relatively respectable rate of growth' although it 'has enjoyed democratic freedom of organisation and security against invasion for some time'. In fact, as one would expect from the theory, it is one of the most densely organised countries of all. The reason why this does not depress its economic performance is, according to Olson, that its interest associations are 'highly centralised' – with the result that 'Swedish labour unions are usually anxious to promote economic growth and that their leaders point out how growth is advantageous to their membership as a whole'. What Olson cannot explain in his model is why this high degree of centralisation should persist against the 'natural' pluralist pressures for fragmentation, decentralisation, and specialisation of organised interests.

The key to the problem may be in Olson's concept of the role of the State in general and in his concepts of democracy and the freedom to organise in particular. At the end of his paper, Olson suggests that there may be 'a most disturbing "internal contradiction" in the evolution of the developed democracies', namely, the contradiction 'between our desire for democratic stability and peace, on the one hand, and our desire for realising our full economic potential, on the other'. Obviously, this contradiction must appear the more unsolvable the more 'democracy' is identified with non-interference by the State in the organisation of producer interests – in effect, with a pluralist pattern of interest representation. The typical case of a State that is democratic in this sense is the British State as it relates to the British system of industrial relations. The abstention of the State in Britain from attempting to regulate the organisation and accommodation of industrial interests, and the resulting voluntary character of the industrial relations system, permit an unlimited growth of organised interests along Olson's 'natural' pattern of pluralist fragmentation and sectionalism. The consequence, according to Olson, is increasingly powerful resistance by small, well-entrenched groups against industrial change, and thus democracy indeed results in deadlock, 'institutional arthritis', and subsequent economic stagnation and decline. However, this would be different if democratic States could acquire a legitimate capacity to intervene in the formation of interest organisations and prevent them from taking their 'natural' course. If a democratic State, without ceasing to be democratic, were able to make the organisational structure of economic interests more centralised and comprehensive – if, in other words, political democracy and corporatist regulation of interest representation could coexist – the contradiction between democracy and economic efficiency would, at least in principle, no longer exist.[3] As we have shown, it is indeed mainly through various mechanisms of State 'institutional design' that German industrial unions are protected from disintegrating into sectional groups pursuing their particular interests on their own and at the expense of others. The same applies, *mutatis mutandis*, to Sweden or Austria. In fact, it can be argued that in most societies, the only force that can effectively prevent pluralist fragmentation of organised interests is the State, and if a pluralist system of interest representation is to be avoided or transformed, the choice is not between a voluntary and a State-interventionist approach but just between different forms of State intervention.

To sum up, the cure for 'institutional arthritis', and the economic stagnation resulting from it, in democratic societies like Sweden or West Germany is intervention by the State not so much in the economy as such but rather in the organisation of collective economic interests. The reason why Britain has a pluralist system of industrial relations that tends to resist change and adjustment, while West Germany has a much more corporatist one, is the different role played by the State in the two societies. While the British State, in industry even more than elsewhere, has always refrained from interfering with private interest organisations, the German State has traditionally been much more activist in this respect. In this tradition, the State in the Federal Republic acts in a variety of ways as a supporting, facilitating, encouraging force in the formation and preservation of broad, encompassing, internally heterogenous interest organisations. Ironically, but hardly unintended, the interventionist policy of the German State on the organisational forms of social interests enables it in many cases to abstain from direct economic intervention since it provides interest groups with a capacity to find viable solutions between and for themselves. This was the case in the example of the S1 redundancy scheme at Volkswagen whose considerable political problems could be defused within the system of functional representation (that is, the industrial relations system) and, unlike the British Leyland crisis in the early 1970s, never required the government to accept direct responsibility for finding a solution. Corporatist 'institutional design', in other words, may make it possible for governments to protect themselves from being 'overloaded', whereas pluralist non-interference in organisational structures may result in excessive demand for authoritative decisions and subsequent 'State failure'.

The State and the limits of institutional design

Assuming that corporatist systems of industrial relations do indeed allow for greater economic efficiency, and assuming further that the differences between pluralist and corporatist institutional structures are to a significant extent accounted for by different degree of State regulation, the question arises whether and how a government whose economic policies are frustrated by pluralistic group interests can reorganise such interests in a corporatist mould. It is not surprising that this question, in one form or another, has been frequently and intensely discussed in Britain during the past two decades. Especially in the late 1960s and early 1970s, comparisons between the British industrial relations system and the systems of other, more successful countries were very fashionable, and the problem of whether a society can learn from another and re-design some of its political institutions accordingly was widely debated. More than anything else, discussions centred on the problem of whether British governments, like governments in Germany, Austria and Sweden, should give up their non-interference in industrial relations and involve themselves directly in the organisation and accommodation of industrial interests. Although much has happened since, the argument on this cannot yet be considered closed, and it may be useful to add a few thoughts on the basis of the material presented in this study.

The basic problem for British governments in trying to transform the industrial relations system into a corporatist one is that the role of the State as an agent of social change and social control is itself a fundamental structural property of a society and it cannot easily be changed by government action. In countries like Germany and Sweden, the State has for centuries been deeply involved in many aspects of social life, and its early and continuing involvement in industrial relations conformed to a long established general pattern. The British State, by comparison, was always relatively weak, and it was probably weakest in the formative period of the modern system of industrial relations in the nineteenth century. This weakness, it could be argued, is bound to be self-perpetuating. For a State that does not already have considerable authority over its society – and is in fact seen by the latter more as 'public enemy number one' than as the legitimate representative of the common weal – the formidable task of redesigning a system of organised interests may be just too ambitious. The conclusion would be that since the creation by government action of a strong role for the State in the organisation of industrial interests presupposes the very role that is to be created, it is logically and what is more, practically impossible.

There are indications that this conclusion is realistic. Especially since the disaster of the 1971 Industrial Relations Act, it is more than ever the prevailing opinion in Britain that 'legal regulation of industrial relations does not work here', and that State reform of and State involvement in industrial relations is, if not necessarily undesirable, thoroughly unmanageable. On the other hand, although the practical conclusion is likely to remain unchanged, it is questionable whether the 1971 Industrial Relations Act can be cited as evidence against the application to British conditions of a German form of State intervention in industrial relations. In at least two important respects, the approach chosen by the authors of the 1971 Industrial Relations Act differed from the German approach, and it may be useful to outline these differences briefly if only to clarify further the way neo-corporatist industrial relations systems function.

First, German labour law does provide for punitive sanctions against trade unions and their leaders if important rules are violated. But these sanctions are not central to the system, and they are above all embedded in an elaborate framework of positive incentives. The reason why the rule of law is accepted in German industrial relations is not the disadvantages it creates for non-conformers but the advantages it offers to conformers. As far as the labour side is concerned, these advantages are not just a codification of powers unions already have or can gain on their own, but are newly created through legal intervention and add to the means of action unions have available. The most important of such positive incentives is industrial democracy. Co-determination and the acceptance of State concertation and regulation are intimately linked with each other. German unions accept State regulation of industrial relations as legitimate because one of its main outcomes is the institutionalisation of trade union influence on economic and organisational decisions in the individual enterprise. The main reason why legal veto powers of works councils and the presence of union representatives on supervisory boards are so important for trade unions is that they give them confidence that employers will, and can be made to, stand by negotiated understandings. Co-operative behaviour on the part of trade unions often involves foregoing short-term advantages in favour of long-term benefits. But this unions can do only if they can be reasonably sure that such benefits will not be withheld later, and one way of reassuring them on this point is by granting them institutionalised influence on the management of the enterprise.

Industrial democracy is achieved in a very elementary sense at the expense of the employers who have to share some of their management prerogatives with trade union representatives. In a legally regulated system, the possible adverse effects of this on economic performance are limited, if not compensated for, by the fact that union interference with managerial discretion takes an identical and predictable form throughout the economy and is subject to judicial review. Nevertheless from the perspective of employers, industrial democracy, apart from the economic costs it entails, constitutes a fundamental intrusion on their status as wielders of property-based powers and privileges. Whatever the benefits the works constitution may create for him, a German employer confronted with a skilled works council has ceased to be *Herr im Hause*, and to many this may appear a high price to pay for the advantages of concerted, neo-corporatist industrial relations. Legal regulation of industrial relations that relies primarily on punitive sanctions against trade unions but which is not linked to some form of industrial democracy and union organisational privileges would fail in Germany just as it failed in Britain in the early 1970s. A government that tries to curtail union autonomy but is unwilling to curtail managerial autonomy at the same time might as well forget about neo-corporatism: the chances that its efforts at 'institutional design' will be successful are nil.

Second, State intervention in trade union organisational structures in West Germany is entirely by indirect means. There is no Trade Unions Act in West Germany, and a law prescribing the internal structures of trade unions would probably be no more enforceable than was the 1971

Industrial Relations Act. Whatever influence there is by the law on the organisational structure of German trade unions – and as has been shown, this influence is indeed considerable – works only indirectly through non-union institutions such as the works council, co-determination, the Labour Court system and so on. The success of these institutions in contributing to the establishment and protection of a system of monopolistic industrial unions – which in turn constitutes a major precondition for the viability of corporatist State intervention and concertation – is to an important degree due to the fact that officially such institutions have nothing to do with trade unions structures at all. State influence on the structure of trade union organisation in Germany works primarily through informal rewards for organisational restructuring and through the creation and satisfaction of vested organisational interests. It is only if a government is prepared to rely on such indirect forms of organisational design that it can hope to exercise a lasting influence on trade union structures.

If the State cannot be counted upon as an agent of institutional reform, who can? There is no reason to believe that a voluntary reorganisation of the British industrial relations system in a corporatist pattern is any more likely than a State-guided one. While examples of 'societal corporatism' do exist – a case in point would be Switzerland – they are rare and require highly special circumstances. As far as Britain is concerned, it is difficult to imagine how the traditional pattern of unregulated, State-free interaction between industrial interests could produce anything fundamentally different from the existing institutional arrangement. In fact, it can safely be predicted that, in the future no less than in the past, the call for the voluntary reform of industrial relations will result in nothing but the continuation of the present structure, and for this reason it will continue to be the slogan of those who either feel comfortable with the existing situation or have given up any hope of changing it.

The conclusion to which these considerations lead is clear. If neither the State nor the social groups themselves are capable of creating corporatist institutions of industrial interest intermediation, such institutions will not come about. It is conceivable that there are societies that, for whatever reason, have not and cannot acquire the capacity to develop corporatist structures, and Britain with its long liberal tradition could indeed be such a society. The question is, of course, whether this means that there is no way out of the 'pluralist deadlock', and whether it implies that the problems this deadlock poses for industrial change and adjustment – Olson's 'institutional arthritis' – are incurable. In the last part of this chapter, it will be argued that if there is no neo-corporatist solution to economic stagnation, there may, under certain conditions, be a neo-liberal one, and if the considerable social costs which this solution entails are discounted it could be even more effective than its corporatist alternative.

Corporatism, pluralism and economic performance

It has already been suggested that, *ceteris paribus*, economies or industries with a corporatist system of interest intermediation can be expected to be more efficient because, among other things, broad, encompassing trade unions do not find it in their interest to demand job control and job ownership for small groups of their members if this would entail a general loss in economic performance. For the protection of workers who may be negatively affected by technological change, unions that are organised in a corporatist fashion tend to prefer solutions that do not interfere with the industry's flexibility and its capacity for rationalisation and adjustment. Whether or not such strategies can be found depends not least on the presence of a supportive government social policy and labour market policy (high unemployment insurance payments, adequate investment in re-training, and an active industrial policy). To the extent that union flexibility improves economic performance, it makes it possible for the unions to gain high real wages for their members, and for the State to increase or maintain its expenditure on social and labour market policy measures. Both, in turn, add to the capacity of trade union leaders to fend off demands by individual groups of members for more defensive reactions to rationalisation and thus help to maintain the unions' commitment to change and flexibility. The consequence is a self-sustaining process – a virtuous circle – in which economic performance and trade union co-operation in rationalisation continually reinforce each other.

The opposite picture emerges in a pluralist system. By defending the immediate, particularistic interests of their small, narrowly defined constituencies in relation to industrial change, pluralist unions create rigidities in the organisation of work and production that reduce their industry's capacity to adjust. The consequence is diminishing economic performance, stagnating or declining real wages, narrow financial limits to state social policy, fewer employment alternatives for workers who lose their jobs in the course of industrial change, and unemployment. As a result, there is an increased probability that the costs of change and mobility will have to be borne by the individual workers themselves rather than the community at large. Unfortunately the more unlikely it is that workers affected by change will find adequate alternative employment,[4] the negative attitude of trade unions towards change will be confirmed, and demands by members for protection will become even stronger. The result may be a further decline in economic performance. Thus, in the same way in which the dynamic of a corporatist industrial relations system can be characterised as a virtuous circle of union co-operation and economic growth, so the typical dynamic of a pluralist system may be a vicious circle of union resistance to change and economic decline.

These are 'ideal' models, only, however, and although they resemble in many respects the experience in Germany and Britain, they should not be confused with reality. The way of making the models more complex and, perhaps, more realistic is by speculating about the conditions under which the two circles might break. As far as the vicious circle of pluralism is concerned, it has been pointed out that the veto powers and immunities of pluralist sectional groups are not formally established in law but are solely based on each group's market and bargaining power. If this power were to decline below a certain threshold, there would be nothing that would prevent employers revoking whatever rights and privileges they were forced to concede under earlier, less favourable circumstances. One way in which the bargaining power of organised labour can be weakened is through unemployment, and an important cause of unemployment is delayed industrial adjustment and low productivity. This hints at the possibility of cyclical change. Trade unions in pluralist industrial relations systems may, in periods of economic growth and high demand for labour, be able to force upon employers manning agreements, employment guarantees, and other restrictive practices. However, the economic decline and unemployment will undercut the unions' bargaining power and strengthen that of the employers. When the crisis has become deep enough, employers will be able to disregard whatever union resistance is left, and reorganise the industry on their own terms. Indeed, there are indications that this is what is happening in Britain at the present time.

Even under the auspices of pluralism, however, it is to be expected that an important part in such a development will be played by the State. Unions that restrict industrial performance are not weakened in their bargaining power if they can get the government of the day to create artificial full employment by subsidisation and/or inflation. As long as government policy follows the 'full employment imperative' of modern welfare state politics, and as long as it can do so with some success and without a collapse of the currency, pluralist unions can continue to build considerable (defensive) power. But this is not likely to go on forever. A government that attempts to deliver full employment to the unions without being able to get their co-operation on incomes and, more importantly, industrial adjustment, runs the risk of being eventually overtaken by another government which makes the fight against inflation its main objective and refuses to underwrite the unemployment consequences of autonomous, unconcerted collective bargaining. At this point, the union privileges and immunities established under full employment begin to dissolve under the pressure of changed market conditions and power relations.

It is obvious that this scenario comes close to the situation in Britain before and after the change of government in 1979. The fundamental and in fact unsolvable problem of the Labour Government between 1974 and 1979 was that the unions expected it to provide for full employment without being prepared to make significant concessions on their established privilege of free collective bargaining. The accession to power of the Conservatives in 1979 represented a radically new attempt by the State to escape from this perennial trap. Unlike the Labour Government, the Conservatives no longer undertook to intervene in collective bargaining. In this respect, their policy is just what British trade unions have time and again asked for whatever party has been in power. At the same time, the Conservative government argues that if the unions want sole responsibility for bargaining, they must also accept responsibility for its outcome. While this point has been made by many others in the past, the Thatcher government for the first time has done what most theorists and practitioners of modern politics would have believed impossible: it has disassociated itself from the seemingly categoric imperative of full employment. Given that British trade unions never accepted the idea that if the State is to bear responsibility for the labour market, it must have a say in collective bargaining – and not only on incomes but also on manpower use – this is not an illogical response. The reason why it looks so extraordinary is that many, including most trade union leaders, have come to believe that in a democratic society, the State has no choice but to pursue a full employment policy and that therefore unions, if only they are stubborn enough, can get the best of two worlds: nineteenth-century liberalism (and voluntarism), and twentieth-century State interventionism.

The idea behind a policy that makes the unions, and even more so their members, feel the unemployment consequences of pluralist collective bargaining is obvious. The deeper the crisis, the more the employers can afford to take a hard line in negotiations on change and rationalisation, cut out unions from consultation, reaffirm managerial prerogatives, withdraw organisational privileges, disregard work rules and manning agreements, dismiss union representatives, and so on. With shop floor power waning and union influence not protected by a legal institutional framework, employers might in a relatively short time be able to 'roll back' union positions that have been built up over decades.[5] If this occurs on a sufficiently large scale, it may result in what may be called a neo-liberal cure to institutional arthritis – a solution of accumulated problems of adjustment through the forces of the (labour) market rather than through negotiated compromise.[6] Provided that the crisis is deep enough, so that union resistance is effectively wiped out, the pluralist organisation of industrial relations could at this point cease to be an impediment to economic performance and could in fact begin to constitute a competitive advantage.

There is no doubt that the costs of a neo-liberal therapy are tremendous. On the other hand, if a corporatist solution is not available, neo-liberalism may be the only alternative left – although its success is by no means guaranteed. (While institutional factors do affect economic success, there are other factors that may in certain conditions be more powerful.) Costs are incurred by a neo-liberal strategy in at least two respects. While it is in principle conceivable that a roll-back of trade unionism can restore flexibility and efficiency to an economy, this may be possible in a democratic society only at the expense of millions of people who for months and years are forced out of employment. Other costs will be incurred if and when the patient survives the cure and recovers. Just as employers in pluralist systems are not prevented from taking advantage of trade union weakness in a crisis, trade unions are not restrained in using all the power they have in periods of prosperity. If a neo-liberal strategy should indeed lead to economic recovery, the unions are likely to present in full the unpaid bills from the crisis and, in addition, will do their utmost to establish even stronger privileges and immunities than before. At this point, if the opportunity for co-operative institution-building in a time of joint distress has been missed, the cycle will begin again and the creeping disease will re-appear.

The breaking point of the virtuous circle of corporatism, unlike the origins of economic decay in pluralist systems, lies not in periods of prosperity but in times of economic recession. Within the confines of a simplified model, corporatist prosperity is self-sustaining and there is no intrinsic reason for trade unions to reconsider their positive attitude on industrial change. The situation becomes different, however, if exogenous factors which impair the system's economic performance are allowed for. Such factors include increased competitiveness of other systems, rising prices of raw materials, high international interest rates, and turbulence in the world monetary system. If such developments reduce employment and especially if they reduce the chances of mobile workers finding new jobs, unions may come under increasing pressure from members seeking improved protection in their present jobs and if this pressure becomes strong enough, even broad and monopolistic industrial unions may not be able fully to disregard it. One restrictive agreement in favour of a particular group of workers will lead to demands for similar agreements by other groups, and since trade union bargaining power in corporatist systems is less dependent on the market than in pluralist systems, such agreements may in fact be gained. The more this tendency proliferates, the more the flexibility of the economy and, as a result, its performance and external competitiveness will suffer. Insofar as this gives rise to further demands for protection by union members, the virtuous circle may at this point turn into a vicious circle of the kind already described.

One possible exogenous cause of economic decline in corporatist systems may be the improved performance of pluralist competitors after a neo-liberal 'roll-back'. While corporatist systems do adjust more swiftly and more efficiently than deadlocked pluralist systems, it may be difficult for them to compete with a 'purged' pluralism that has restored the market and capital to their controlling position. (On the assumption, of course, that a neo-liberal recovery is possible at all and that unions in a liberal-pluralist system can, for a sufficient period of time, be prevented from taking advantage of the recovery; this is probably an unrealistic assumption.) Social partnership, whatever its advantages, entails costs that, unlike the costs of a neo-liberal purge, show up in the books of individual employers. Negotiated change and adaptation are certainly better than none but they are more expensive and probably proceed at a slower pace than change dictated by employers on exclusive terms. As the first two case studies in particular demonstrated, the outcome of corporatist intermediation of industrial interests tends to be a compromise that is economically suboptimal – perhaps not from the perspective of society as a whole but certainly from that of the individual firm. A corporatist economy in which unions have enough institutionalised influence to ensure that employers have to internalise at least part of the social costs of restructuring, may have a hard time competing with pluralist economies in which employers have been able to rationalise production by wiping out trade union influence and lowering the standards and conditions of work.

Relatively declining economic performance of corporatist systems, for whatever reasons, may undermine their institutional stability. Disintegrative tendencies are more likely to emanate from the employers than from the unions. Especially in an export-oriented economy, unions do not have much of a rational alternative to continued co-operation in industrial adjustment. In a severe economic crisis, even West German trade unions may succumb to the attraction of ideological politics and illusory expectations. But it is more likely, given their organisational structure and the long-term interests of their members, that they will be able to resist demands from members for pluralist protection. The situation is different with the employers who, faced with the declining market power of trade unions, may begin to wonder whether the corporatist limitation of managerial discretion through institutionalised union influence has not become too high a price to pay for workers' acceptance of change (not to speak of the economic costs that negotiated change entails). The greater, as a result of the crisis, the gap between the market power and the influence of trade unions through corporatist institutions, the more likely employers are to see 'social partnership' as part of the problem itself, rather than as a solution to the problem of industrial change. Not least among the factors that create what might be called a 'neo-liberal temptation'[7] for employers in economically declining corporatist systems, is the example which might be given by employers in competing pluralist systems taking advantage of the crisis to restore their industrial hegemony and re-establish discretionary managerial powers.

On the other hand, a complete roll-back of trade union influence would not be easy to achieve in a corporatist system even in conditons of economic crisis. Corporatist institutions, once established, make it difficult for their constituent parts to regain their previous autonomy. This applies to the interests of employers no less than to those of workers. Thus, one characteristic of corporatism is that it allows for relatively little internal structural variation. The legal regulation of industrial relations in West Germany narrowly limits the possibility of gradual systemic change starting at the level of individual plants or industries. In Britain union organisational privileges, including union recognition, can in principle be withdrawn by any individual private employer, the local distribution of power permitting. In this way, such privileges can, step by step and without much public attention, be eliminated for entire industries or regions. In West Germany, on the other hand, a change to institutional neo-liberalism would require at a very early stage an amendment of the 1972 Works Constitution Act and the 1976 Co-Determination Act. Any serious attempt at such an amendment would put the country's basic social and political consensus in jeopardy and would give rise to a deeply divisive, society-wide and from the beginning highly politicised conflict the effects of which would be incalculable. Moreover, in corporatist systems employers as well as workers have strong associations that represent the long-term interests of their members not only to other groups or to the State but also to the members themselves. Like trade unions in a time of economic prosperity, employers associations during a crisis have good strategic reasons for preventing their members from using their market power to the full. By impressing on their membership that the situation may be reversed and that unless institutional safeguards are created or protected, the other side will then take revenge, employers associations promote not only important interests of their members but also their own organisational interest in stable bargaining relations. The stronger such associations are, the more likely it is that changes in the market positions of trade unions and employers will not lead to an institutional crisis.

In the end, the real difference between a corporatist and a pluralist system of industrial relations may not be that the former is more economically efficient but that it provides for more steadiness and predictability in the interaction between unions and employers, less cyclical fluctuation of relative power, and more gradual rather than catastrophic processes of adaptation and adjustment. Just as a 'solidaristic' wage policy is intended to spread increases in real incomes more evenly over the workforce regardless of differences of individual market position, corporatist institutions tend to hold the influence of trade unions on managerial decisions relatively constant over time regardless of the business cycle. As a result, the need for, and the price of, negotiated as distinguished from unilaterally imposed industrial change are kept relatively insensitive to medium-term (labour) market fluctuations. While this may in most circumstances increase the costs of adaptation and rationalisation for individual firms, it contributes to containing the social costs of economic change by providing for a more stable, more long-term oriented and, on the whole, more generally acceptable accommodation of conflicting interests.

Summary
This study has attempted to show how the structure of industrial interest representation, trade union influence on managerial decisions, and responsible trade union policies are related to each other. The final chapter has suggested the concept of 'neo-corporatism' to denote the German syndrome of encompassing trade unionism and collective bargaining, institutionalised power sharing between management and representatives of the workforce, and 'social partnership'. The working of this arrangement was illustrated by three detailed case studies. The final chapter has also tried to lay out some of the choices the State and organised industrial interests in advanced economies face in designing and institutionalising their mutual relationships as parties to 'joint regulation'. For this purpose it has introduced a continuum between a corporatist and a pluralist mode of industrial interest politics and Britain, in comparison to Germany, was found to be much closer to the pluralist end of the continuum. Which of the various options between the two ends will be realised in a given historical situation depends on the outcome of a complex interplay of many different forces and factors. Among other things, the realised option will be conditioned by the structures and potential for change of the institutions of industrial relations that already exist. It is to an improved understanding of these institutions that the present study has attempted to make a contribution.

156   *Industrial Relations in West Germany*

Footnotes

1   Ph.C. Schmitter, Still the Century of Corporatism? *The Review of Politics*, 36, 1974, pp. 85–131.

2   Ibid., pp. 93–4.

3   Olson himself seems to believe that this is possible. To resolve the contradiction between democracy and economic efficiency, he suggests that the State should intervene in the organisation of private interests by providing 'assistance (to) groups, such as consumers, that are under-represented, and by legislation designed to countervail the harmful effects of groups with monopoly power or disproportionate political organisation'. See M. Olson, The Political Economy of Comparative Growth Rates in *US Economic Growth from 1976 to 1986: Prospects, Problems and Patterns*, Studies prepared for the use of the Joint Economic Committee of the Congress of the United States, p. 39.

4   This will generally be difficult, quite apart from the overall economic situation, in a system which has strong seniority rights, rigid demarcations between occupations and established forms of individual or collective job ownership. The more groups of workers succeed in establishing institutionalised employment privileges, the lower the chances of mobile workers of finding a job and the greater the need for them to gain privileges of their own.

5   The following extract from the *Financial Times* of 2 June 1981, illustrates the point. 'BL's cars division intends to end the 30-year-old system under which senior shop stewards and convenors spend all their time on union work. The proposal was made during talks on the new draft procedure agreement. It would bring the 100 or more full time senior stewards under management discipline, to be allocated work when they are not engaged in union business. The company told representatives of its four white-collar unions that it wants to push through the changes at plant level. . . . Both national and local (union) officials see the move as part of a general 'union-bashing' climate in the company. In a leaflet distributed to Longbridge workers, TGWU stewards say: 'no one can be in any doubt that BL management is using the current weakness in trade union organisation (to tear down positions) built up over years of strength and embodied in current arguments. . .' BL yesterday denied that the measure was aimed at weakening the unions. The company said it was an attempt to construct a 'disciplined approach to bargaining'. (*Financial Times*, June 2, 1981)

6   'Sir Michael Edwardes, chairman of loss-making BL, disclosed a new set of productivity figures yesterday showing that the company is now making more cars with 30,000 fewer workers than a year ago . . . Sir Michael said that since the start of 1978 more than 60,000 people had left the company, making BL's total United Kingdom labour force 120,000 and that demanning had not caused a single major strike. Thirteen factories had been totally or partly closed . . . Sir Michael has already indicated that numbers (of workers) will continue to fall until the end of next year . . . Sir Michael said in 1976 the big BL factory at Longbridge was free of disputes for only 8 per cent of working hours. Now the company had been dispute-free in its 36 factories this year for

more than 99 per cent of available hours.' Extract from *The Times*, 18 June, 1981.

[7] Paraphrasing a concept of Schmitter, op. cit.

Appendix: Excerpts from the Works Constitution Act 1972

PART I GENERAL PROVISIONS

1 Establishment of works councils

Works councils shall be elected in all establishment (Betriebe) that normally have five or more permanent employees with voting rights, including three who are eligible.

2 Status of trade unions and employers' associations

(1) The employer and the works council shall work together in a spirit of mutual trust having regard to the applicable collective agreements and in co-operation with the trade unions and employers' associations represented in the establishment for the good of the employees and of the establishment.

(3) This Act shall not affect the functions of trade unions and employers' associations and more particularly the protection of their members' interests.

9 Number of members of works council

The membership of the works council shall be as follows, according to the number of employees with voting rights normally employed in the establishment:

5 to 20 employees :	1 person (works representative)
21 to 50 employees :	3 members
51 to 150 employees :	5 members
151 to 300 employees :	7 members
301 to 600 employees :	9 members
601 to 1,000 employees :	11 members
1,001 to 2,000 employees :	15 members
2,001 to 3,000 employees :	19 members
3,001 to 4,000 employees :	23 members
4,001 to 5,000 employees :	27 members
5,001 to 7,000 employees :	29 members
7,001 to 9,000 employees :	31 members

In establishments employing more than 9,000 employees the number of members of the works council shall be increased by two members for every additional fraction of 3,000 employees.

10 Representation of minority groups

(1) Wage earners and salaried employees shall be represented according to their relative numerical strength whenever the works council consists of three or more members.

(2) The minimum representation of the minority group shall be as follows, according to the number of persons the group comprises:

up to 50 persons	1 representative
51 to 200 persons	2 representatives
201 to 600 persons	3 representatives
601 to 1,000 persons	4 representatives
1,001 to 3,000 persons	5 representatives
3,001 to 5,000 persons	6 representatives
5,001 to 9,000 persons	7 representatives
9,001 to 15,000 persons	8 representatives
over 15,000 persons	9 representatives

(3) Minority groups shall not be represented if the group comprises five or less employees constituting not more than one-twentieth of all the employees in the establishment.

12 Different allocation of seats

(1) The proportion of seats on the works council allocated to each group may differ from that prescribed by section 10 if both groups so decide by separate secret ballots held before the election.

(2) Persons belonging to one group may also be elected by the other group. If so, the persons so elected shall be deemed for these purposes to be members of the group that elected them. The foregoing shall also apply to substitutes.

14 Election procedure

(1) The works council shall be elected directly by secret ballot.

(5) Employees with voting rights shall be entitled to submit lists of candidates for the works council elections. Each list of candidates shall be signed by at least one-tenth of the voting members of the group, but not by less than three members with voting rights. The signatures of 100 members of the group shall be sufficient in all cases.

20 Protection against obstruction and costs of the election

(1) No person shall obstruct the election of a works council. In particular no employee shall be restricted in his right to vote or to stand for election.

(2) Any attempt to influence a works council election by inflicting or threatening any unfavourable treatment or by granting or promising any advantage shall be unlawful.

(3) The costs of the election shall be borne by the employer. Any loss of working time entailed by voting or candidature or the performance of duties on the electoral board shall not give the employer a right to reduce the remuneration.

31 Attendance of trade union delegates

If one-fourth of the members or the majority of a group represented on the works council so request, a delegate of a trade union represented on the works council may be invited to attend meetings in an advisory capacity; in that case the trade union shall be notified in good time of the time of the meeting and its agenda.

37 Honorary nature of post; loss of working time

(1) The post of member of the works council shall be unpaid.

(2) The members of the works council shall be released from their work duties without loss of pay to the extent necessary for the proper performance of their functions, having regard to the size and nature of the establishment.

(4) During his term of office and for one year thereafter the remuneration of a member of the works council shall not be fixed at a lower rate than the remuneration paid to workers in a comparable position who have followed the career that is usual in the establishment. The same shall apply to general benefits granted by the employer.

(6) Subsection (2) shall apply, *mutatis mutandis*, to the attendance of training and educational courses, in so far as the knowledge imparted is necessary for the activities of the works council. In scheduling the time for attending training and educational courses the works council shall take account of the operational requirements of the establishment. It shall notify the employer in good time of the attendance of training and educational courses and of the time at which they are held. If the employer feels that the operational requirements of the establishment have not sufficiently been taken into account, he may submit the case to the conciliation committee. The award of the conciliation committee shall take the place of an agreement between the employer and the works council.

(7) Without prejudice to subsection (6), each member of the works council shall be entitled during his regular term of office to a paid release for a total of three weeks to enable him to attend training and educational courses that have been approved for this purpose by the competent central labour authority of the Land concerned after consultation with the central organisation of trade unions and employers'

associations. The entitlement conferred by the preceding sentence shall be increased to four weeks where the employee is serving for the first time as a member of either the works council or a youth delegation. The second to fifth sentences of the preceding subsection shall apply.

38 Releases

(1) The minimum number of works council members to be released from their work duties shall depend on the number of employees normally employed in the establishment, as set out below:

300 to	600	employees	1	member of the works council
600 to	1,000	employees	2	members of the works council
1,001 to	2,000	employees	3	members of the works council
2,001 to	3,000	employees	4	members of the works council
3,001 to	4,000	employees	5	members of the works council
4,001 to	5,000	employees	6	members of the works council
5,001 to	6,000	employees	7	members of the works council
6,001 to	7,000	employees	8	members of the works council
7,001 to	8,000	employees	9	members of the works council
8,001 to	9,000	employees	10	members of the works council
9,001 to	10,000	employees	11	members of the works council

In establishments with more than 10,000 employees one further member of the works council shall be released for each additional fraction of 2,000 employees. Other arrangements concerning release can be made by collective or works agreement.

(2) Decisions on releases shall be taken by the works council after consultation with the employer. Due account shall be taken of the groups. If each group on the works council constitutes more than one-third of its total membership, each group shall decide on its own which of its members on the works council are to benefit from the release. The works council shall give the employer the names of the members to be released. If the employer feels that the decision is not justified by the facts he may appeal to the conciliation committee within two weeks of being notified. The award of the conciliation committee shall take the place of an agreement between the employer and the works council. If the employer does not appeal to the conciliation committee, the decision shall take effect on the expiry of the two weeks referred to above.

(3) In respect of members of the works council who have been released from their work duties for three full consecutive terms of office, the period during which their remuneration shall continue to be governed by section 37 (4) and their employment by section 37 (5) shall be extended to two years after the expiry of their term of office.

(4) Members of the works council who have been released from their work duties shall not be debarred from vocational training programmes inside or outside the establishment. Within a year of the date on which the release comes to an end, members of the works council shall be allowed, as far as the facilities offered by the establishment permit, to take any career training normally provided for the employees of the establishment that they missed because of their release. In respect of members of the works council who were released from their work duties for three full consecutive terms of office, the period referred to in the preceding sentence shall be extended to two years.

40 Expenses of the works council and material facilities

(1) Any expenses arising out of the activities of the works council shall be defrayed by the employer.

(2) The employer shall provide to the necessary extent the premises, material facilities and office staff required for the meetings, consultations and day-to-day operation of the works council.

PART IV COLLABORATION BY EMPLOYEES AND CO-DETERMINATION

74 Principles of collaboration

(1) The employer and the works council shall meet together at least once a month for joint conferences. They shall discuss the matters at issue with an earnest desire to reach agreement and make suggestions for settling their differences.

(2) Acts of industrial warfare between the employer and the works council shall be unlawful; the foregoing shall not apply to industrial disputes between collective bargaining parties. The employer and the works council shall refrain from activities that interfere with operations or imperil the tranquillity of the establishment. They shall refrain from any activity within the establishment in promotion of a political party; the foregoing shall not apply to dealing with matters of direct concern to the establishment or its employees in the field of collective bargaining policy, social policy and of a financial nature.

(3) The fact that an employee has assumed duties under this Act shall not restrict him in his trade union activities even where such activities are carried out in the establishment.

75 Principles for the treatment of persons employed in the establishment

(1) The employer and the works council shall ensure that every person employed in the establishment is treated in accordance with the prin-

ciples of law and equity and in particular that there is no discrimination against persons on account of their race, creed, nationality, origin, political or trade union activity or convictions, or sex. They shall make sure that employees do not suffer any prejudice because they have exceeded a certain age.

(2) The employer and the works council shall safeguard and promote the untrammelled development of the personality of the employees of the establishment.

76 Conciliation committee

(1) Whenever the need arises a conciliation committee shall be set up for the purpose of settling differences of opinion between the employer and the works council, central works council or combine works council. A standing conciliation committee may be established by works agreement.

(2) The conciliation committee shall be composed of assessors appointed in equal number by the employer and the works council and of an independent chairman accepted by both sides. If no agreement can be reached on a chairman, he shall be appointed by the Labour Court. The latter shall also decide in cases where no agreement can be reached on the number of assessors.

(3) The conciliation committee shall adopt its decisions by majority vote after oral proceedings. The chairman shall not participate in the voting; in the case of a tie the discussion shall be resumed and the chairman shall participate in the subsequent vote. The decisions of the conciliation committee shall be recorded in writing, signed by the chairman and transmitted to the employer and the works council.

(5) In cases where the award of the conciliation committee takes the place of an agreement between the employer and the works council, the conciliation committee shall act at the request of either side. If one side fails to appoint members or if the members appointed by one side fail to attend after being convened in due time, the chairman and the members present shall make the award without following the procedure laid down in subsection (3). In taking its decisions the conciliation committee shall have due regard to the interests of the establishment and of the employees concerned as reasonably assessed. The employer of the works council may make an appeal to the Labour Court on the grounds that the conciliation committee has exceeded its powers, but only within two weeks of the date of notification of the award.

77 Execution of joint decisions, works agreements

(1) Agreements between the works council and the employer including those based on an award of the conciliation committee shall be executed by the employer save where otherwise agreed in particular cases. The

works council shall not interfere with the management of the establishment by any unilateral action.

(2) Works agreements shall be negotiated by the works council and the employer and recorded in writing. They shall be signed by both sides, except where they are based on an award of the conciliation committee. The employer shall keep the works agreement in a suitable place in the establishment.

(3) Works agreement shall not deal with remuneration and other conditions of employment that have been fixed or are normally fixed by collective agreement. The foregoing shall not apply where a collective agreement expressly authorises the making of supplementary works agreements.

(4) Works agreements shall be mandatory and directly applicable. Any rights granted to employees under a works agreement cannot be waived except with the agreement of the works council. Such rights cannot be forfeited. Any time limits for invoking these rights shall be valid only in so far as they are laid down by collective or works agreement; the same shall apply to any reduction of the periods provided for the lapsing of rights.

(5) Unless otherwise agreed, works agremeents may be terminated at three months' notice.

(6) After the expiry of a works agreement its provisions shall continue to apply until a fresh agreement is made in respect of all matters in which an award of the conciliation committee may take the place of an agreement between the employer and the works council.

80 General duties
(1) The works council shall have the following general duties:
1. to see that effect is given to Acts, ordinances, safety regulations, collective agreements and works agreements for the benefit of the employees;
2. to make recommendations to the employer for action benefiting the establishment and the staff;
3. to receive suggestions from employees and the youth delegation and, if they are found to be justified, to negotiate with the employer for their implementation; it shall inform the employers concerned of the state of the negotiations and their results;
4. to promote the rehabilitation of disabled persons and other persons in particular need of assistance;
5. to prepare and organise the election of a youth delegation and to collaborate closely with the said delegation in promoting the interests of the young employees; it may invite the youth delegation to make suggestions and to state its views on various matters;
6. to promote the employment of elderly workers in the establishment;

7. to promote the integration of foreign workers in the establishment and to further understanding between them and their German colleagues.

(2) The employer shall supply comprehensive information to the works council in good time to enable it to discharge its duties under this Act. The works council shall, if it so requests, be granted access at any time to any documentation it may require for the discharge of its duties; in this connection the works committee or a committee set up in pursuance of section 28 shall be entitled to inspect the payroll showing the gross wages and salaries of the employees.

(3) In discharging its duties the works council may, after making a more detailed agreement with the employer, call on the advice of experts in as far as the proper discharge of its duties so requires. The experts shall be bound to observe secrecy as prescribed in section 79, *mutatis mutandis*.

87 Right of co-determination

(1) The works council shall have a right of co-determination in the following matters in so far as they are not prescribed by legislation or collective agreement:

1. matters relating to the order by operation of the establishment and the conduct of employees in the establishment;
2. the commencement and termination of the daily working hours including breaks and the distribution of working hours among the days of the week;
3. any temporary reduction or extension of the hours normally worked in the establishment;
4. the time and place for and the form of payment of remuneration;
5. the establishment of general principles for leave arrangements and the preparation of the leave schedule as well as fixing the time at which the leave is to be taken by individual employees, if no agreement is reached between the employer and the employees concerned;
6. the introduction and use of technical devices designed to monitor the behaviour or performance of the employees;
7. arrangements for the prevention of employment accidents and occupational diseases and for the protection of health on the basis of legislation or safety regulations;
8. the form, structuring and administration of social services where scope is limited to the establishment, company or combine;
9. the assignment of and notice to vacate accommodation that is rented to employees in view of their employment relationship as well as the general fixing of the conditions for the use of such accommodation;
10. questions related to remuneration arrangements in the

establishment, including in particular the establishment of principles of remuneration and the introduction and application of new remuneration methods or modification of existing methods;

11. the fixing of job and bonus rates and comparable performance-related remuneration including cash coefficients (i.e. prices per time unit);

12. principles for suggestion schemes in the establishment.

(2) If no agreement can be reached on a matter covered by the preceding subsection, the conciliation committee shall make a decision. The award of the conciliation committee shall take the place of an agreement between the employer and the works council.

90 Information and consultation rights

The employer shall inform the works council in due time of any plans concerning –

1. the construction, alteration or extension of works, offices and other premises belonging to the establishment;

2. technical plant;

3. working process and operations or

4. jobs

and consult the works council on the action envisaged, taking particular account of its impact on the nature of the work and the demands made on the employees. In their consultations the employer and the works council shall have regard to the established findings of ergonomics relating to the tailoring of jobs to meet human requirements.

91 Right of co-determination

Where a special burden is imposed on the employees as a result of changes in jobs, operations or the working environment that are in obvious contradiction to the established findings of ergonomics relating to the tailoring of jobs to meet human requirements, the works council may request appropriate action to obviate, relieve or compensate for the additional stress thus imposed. If no agreement can be reached, the matter shall be decided by the conciliation committee. The award of the conciliation committee shall take the place of an agreement between the employer and the works council.

92 Manpower planning

(1) The employer shall inform the works council in full and in good time of matters relating to manpower planning including in particular present and future manpower needs and the resulting staff movements and vocational training measures and supply the relevant documentation. He shall consult the works council on the nature and extent of the action required and means of avoiding hardship.

99 Co-determination in individual staff movements
(1) In establishments normally employing more than twenty employees with voting rights the employer shall notify the works council in advance of any engagement, grading, regrading and transfer, submit to it the appropriate recruitment documents and in particular supply information on the persons concerned; he shall inform the works council of the implications of the action envisaged, supply it with the necessary supporting documentation and obtain its consent to the action envisaged. In the case of engagements and transfers the employer shall in particular supply information on the job and grading envisaged. Members of the works council shall refrain from divulging any information relating to the personal circumstances and private affairs of the employees concerned that has come to their knowledge in connection with the staff movements referred to in the first and second sentences, where such information is of confidential nature by reason of its implications or content; the second to fourth sentences of section 79(1) shall apply, *mutatis mutandis.*
(2) The works council may refuse its consent in the following cases:
1. if the staff movement would constitute a breach of any Act, ordinance, safety regulation or stipulation of a collective agreement or works agreement, or of a court order or official instruction;
2. if the staff movement would amount to non-observance of a guideline within the meaning of section 95;
3. if there is factual reason to assume that the staff movement is likely to result in the dismissal of or other prejudice to employees of the establishment not warranted by operational or personal reasons;
4. if the employee concerned suffers prejudice through the staff movement although this is not warranted by operational or personal reasons.

102 Co-determination in the case of dismissal
(1) The works council shall be consulted before every dismissal. The employer shall indicate to the works council the reasons for dismissal. Any notice of dismissal that is given without consulting the works council shall be null and void.
(3) The works council may oppose a routine dismissal within the time limit specified in the first sentence of subsection (2) in the following cases:
1. if the employer is selecting the employee to be dismissed disregarded or did not take sufficient account of hardship etc. or such social considerations;
2. if the dismissal would amount to non-observance of a guideline covered by section 95;

3. if the employee whose dismissal is being envisaged could be kept on at another job in the same establishment or in another establishment of the same company;
4. if the employee could be kept on after a reasonable amount of retraining or further training; or
5. if the employee could be kept on after a change in the terms of his contract and he has indicated his agreement to such change.

111 Alterations

In companies that normally have more than twenty employees with voting rights the employer shall inform the works council in full and in good time of any proposed alterations which may entail substantial prejudice to the staff or a large sector thereof and consult the works council on the proposed alterations. The following are alterations within the meaning of the first sentence:

1. reduction of operations in or closure of the whole or important departments of the establishment;
2. transfer of the whole or important departments of the establishment;
3. amalgamation with other establishments;
4. important changes in the organisation, purpose or plant of the establishment;
5. introduction of entirely new work methods and production processes.

112 Reconciliation of interests in the case of alterations; social compensation plans

(1) If the employer and the works council reach an agreement to reconcile their interests in connection with the proposed alterations, the said agreement shall be recorded in writing and signed by the employer and the works council. The foregoing shall also apply to an agreement on full or part compensation for any financial prejudice sustained by staff as a result of the proposed alterations (social compensation plan). The social compensation plan shall have the effect of a works agreement. Section 77 (3) shall not apply to the social compensation plan.

(2) If no reconciliation of interests can be achieved in connection with the proposed alterations or if no agreement is reached on the social compensation plan, the employer or the works council may apply to the president of the Land employment office for mediation. If no such application is made or the attempt at mediation is unsuccessful, the employer or the works council may submit the case to the conciliation committee. The chairman of the conciliation committee may request the president of the Land employment office to take part in the proceedings.

(3) The employer and the works council shall submit proposals to the conciliation committee for the settlement of differences on the reconciliation of interests and the social compensation plan. The conciliation committee shall attempt to reconcile the parties. If an agreement is reached, it shall be recorded in writing and signed by the parties and the chairman.

(4) If no agreement is reached on the social compensation plan, the conciliation committee shall make a decision on the drawing up of a social compensation plan. In doing so, the conciliation committee shall take into account the social interests of the employees concerned while taking care that its decision does not place an unreasonable financial burden on the company. The award of the conciliation committee shall take the place of an agreement between the employer and the works council.

Bibliography

The following list includes recent publications in the English language that deal with West German industrial relations either exclusively or in an internationally comparative perspective. Given the large number of such publications, the list is not intended to be complete. Its purpose is to alert the reader to other, easily available sources from which he or she can get further information on the subject. Other works cited in the text are also listed here.

Adams, J.J. and C.H. Rummel, 1977: 'Workers' Participation in Management in West Germany: Impact on the Worker, the Enterprise and the Trade Union', *Industrial Relations Journal* 8:4–22

Beyme, K. von, 1980: *Challenge to Power: Trade Unions and Industrial Relations in Capitalist Countries*. London: Sage Publications.

C.I.R., 1974: *Worker Participation and Collective Bargaining in Western Europe*, Study 4, London: HMSO.

Clark, J., 1979: 'Concerted Action in the Federal Republic of Germany', *British Journal of Industrial Relations* 18:246–258

Clark, J., H. Hartmann, Ch. Lau, D. Winchester, 1980: *Trade Unions, National Politics and Economic Management: A Comparative Study of the TUC and the DGB*. London: Anglo-German Foundation for the Study of Industrial Society

Clegg, H., 1976: *Trade Unionism Under Collective Bargaining*. Oxford: Basil Blackwell

Cullingford, E.C.M., 1976: *Trade Unions in West Germany*. London: Wilton House Publications

Der Bundesminister für Arbeit und Sozialordnung, 1978: *Co-Determination in the Federal Republic of Germany*. Bonn: Selbstverlag

Hanson, C., Jackson, S., Miller, D., 1981: *The Closed Shop: A Comparative Study in Public Policy and Trade Union Security in Britain, the USA and West Germany*. Aldershot: Gower

Hartmann, H., 1975: 'Co-determination Today and Tomorrow', *British Journal of Industrial Relations* 13, 54–64

Hartmann, H., 1979, 'Works Councils and the Iron Law of Oligarchy'. *British Journal of Industrial Relations*, 18:70–82

Hotz, B., 1982: 'Productivity Differences and Industrial Relations Structures: Engineering Companies in the United Kingdom and the Federal Republic of Germany', *Labour and Society* 333–354

Industrial Democracy Committee, 1976: *Industrial Democracy European Experiences*, London: HMSO

Industrial Democracy in Europe (IDE) International Research Group, 1981: *European Industrial Relations*, Oxford: Oxford University Press

Jacobs, E., Orwell, S., Paterson, P., Weltz, F., 1978: *The Approach to Industrial Change in Britain and Germany*. London: Anglo-German Foundation for the Study of Industrial Society

Kassalow, E.M., 1982: 'Industrial Democracy and Collective Bargaining: A Comparative View', *Labour and Society*, 7, 209–230

Kendall, W., 1975: *The Labour Movement in Europe*, London, Allen Lane

Kerr, C., 1954: 'The Trade Union Movement and the Redistribution of Power in Postwar Germany', *The Quarterly Journal of Economics*, LXVII: 535–64

Martin B., and Kassalow, E.M., eds., 1980: *Labor Relations in Advanced Industrial Societies*, Washington, D.C.; Carnegie Endowment for International Peace

Marsh, A., Heckman, M., Miller, D., 1981: *Workplace Relations in the Engineering Industry in the UK and the Federal Republic of Germany*. London: Anglo-German Foundation for the Study of Industrial Society

Miller, D., 1978; 'Trade Union Workplace Representation in the Federal Republic of Germany: An Analysis of the Postwar Vertrauensleute Policy of the German Metal-Workers' Union (1952–1977)', *British Journal of Industrial Relations* 17:335–54

Miller, D., 1982: 'Social Partnership and the Determinants of Workplace Independence in West Germany', *British Journal of Industrial Relations* 20:44–66

Mitbestimmungskommission, 1970: *Mitbestimmung im Unternehmen*. Stuttgart: Kohlhammer. An English translation was prepared in 1976 by the Legal Research Committee of the Faculty of Law, Queen's University, Belfast

Müller-Jentsch, W., 1981: 'Strikes and Strike Trends in West Germany, 1950–78'. *Industrial Relations Journal* 12:36–57

Müller-Jentsch, W., and Sperling, H.-J., 1978: 'Economic Development, Labour Conflicts and the Industrial Relations System in West Germany'. In: C. Crouch and A. Pizzorno, eds., 1978: *The Resurgence of Class Conflict in Western Europe since 1968*. London: MacMillan, vol. II, 257–306

Olson, M., 1976: 'The political economy of comparative growth rates', in *US Economic Growth from 1976 to 1986: Prospects, Problems and Patterns*. Studies prepared for the use of the Joint Economic Committee of the Congress of the United States, Vol. 2, pp.25—40

Roberts, B.C., ed., 1979: *Towards Industrial Democracy – Europe, Japan and the United States*, Montclair, New Jersey: Allanheld, Osman

Roberts, I.R., 1973: 'The Works Constitution Act and Industrial Relations in West Germany: Implications for the United Kingdom'. *British Journal of Industrial Relations* 11: 349–54

Seglow, P., Streeck, W., Wallace, P., 1982: *Rail Unions in Britain and W. Germany*. London: Policy Studies Institute

Streeck, W., 1981: 'Qualitative Demands and the Neo-Corporatist Manageability of Industrial Relations: Trade Unions and Industrial Relations in West Germany at the Beginning of the Eighties'. *British Journal of Industrial Relations*, 14:149–169

Streeck, W., 1982: 'Organizational Consequences of Corporatist Co-operation in West German Labor Unions', in; G. Lehmbruch and Ph.C. Schmitter, eds., *Patterns of Corporatist Policy-Making*, New York and London: Sage, 29–81

Streeck, W., 1983: Co-Determination: The Fourth Decade. *IIM/LMP* 83–1, Wissenschaftszentrum Berlin. To appear in: *International Yearbook of Organizational Democracy*, vol. II, 'International Perspectives on Organizational Democracy', London: John Wiley and Sons

Streeck, W., Seglow, P., Wallace, P., 1981: 'Competition and Monopoly in Interest Representation', *Organization Studies* 2: 307–330

Streeck, W., and Hoff, A., 1982: Industrial Relations in the German Auto Industry – Developments in the 1970s, *Discussion Paper IIM/LMP 82–25*, Wissenschaftszentrum Berlin

Wilpert, B., 1975; 'Research on Industrial Democracy: The German Case', *Industrial Relations Journal* 5:53–64

Windmuller, J., 1978: 'Workers' Participation in Management in the Federal Republic of Germany', International Institute of Labour Studies, Geneva, *Research Series* No. 32

Index